The Humble Church

D1450936

The Humble Church

Renewing the Body of Christ

Martyn Percy

CANTERBURY
PRESS
Norwich

First published in 2021 by the Canterbury Press Norwich
Editorial office
3rd Floor, Invicta House
108–114 Golden Lane
London EC1Y 0TG, UK
www.canterburypress.co.uk

Canterbury Press is an imprint of Hymns Ancient & Modern Ltd
(a registered charity)

Hymns Ancient & Modern® is a registered trademark of
Hymns Ancient & Modern Ltd
13A Hellesdon Park Road, Norwich,
Norfolk NR6 5DR, UK

Scripture quotations are from the New Revised Standard
Version Bible: Anglicised Edition, copyright © 1989, 1995
National Council of the Churches of Christ in the United States of
America. Used by permission. All rights reserved worldwide.

British Library Cataloguing in Publication data

A catalogue record for this book is available
from the British Library

978-1-78622-315-9

Typeset by Regent Typesetting
Printed and bound by
CPI Group (UK) Ltd

for

Catherine, Sarah,
Sean, Keith, Tony, Desmond and Brian,
Tom, Holy Family Church, Blackbird Leys,
Sext@One and all from T@4

MWP, Epiphany 2021

Contents

Foreword   ix
Gratitude   xi
A Personal Preface   xiii

Beginnings: Down to Earth   1

Part One: Culture and Change

Upside Down, Inside Out   19
A Plague of Numbers   33
New Era – From BC to AC   46

Part Two: Challenge and Church

Mind(ful) – the Generation Gap   61
Abuse, Authority and Authenticity   75
Smoking in Public   89

Part Three: Christ and Christianity

'Us and Them': One Body, One Bread   105
Thy Kingdom Come: Mission and Evangelism   118
Jesus and the Self-Emptying Church   131

Endings: Lowly, Living, Loving   143
Coda: The Stature of Liberty   158

Study Guide for Groups and Individuals   177
Epilogue: No Sign Shall Be Given, Except the
Sign of Jonah   185
Bibliography   191
Endnotes and Further Reading   199
Acknowledgement of Sources   201
Index of Names and Subjects   203

Foreword

It's a good general rule not to slay your prophets because they often turn out to be right. Martyn Percy is one such. He is one of our most perceptive and penetrating theologians, and what he says in this book cannot simply be denied, ignored, or boxed up and put on a shelf. It's too important for that.

The central message is that the church's strategies for growth, handling contentious issues, and generally trying to occupy the high ground, need to be replaced by a determined focus on becoming a humble church with kenotic leadership, following the ways of Jesus and listening attentively to the world. It's a theme that is explored through wide reading and deep cultural engagement. The book is full of telling observations, flashes of wit, fascinating etymology, arresting poetry, and memorable phrases. Martyn Percy doesn't know how to write a dull sentence.

The argument is cool in analysis, passionate in intent, sometimes unfair (it's hard being a bishop), and always engaging. There are tough messages about the church's shortcomings, and some of the generalisations about the church's failure to identify with society's poor and to champion important causes are certainly open to challenge. But the church mustn't escape the sting of what the book reflects back to her.

Martyn is calling faithful Christians to start with God, not with the church. In particular, to start with the God of John 1 and Philippians 2, the God who is *grounded* in incarnation and *emptied* in love for the world. 'Don't do Church; do God' is the author's cry.

This is the voice of a theologian who believes the gospel and loves the church, but is deeply frustrated by institutional inertia and self-preservation. It's a voice to listen to.

The Rt Revd John Pritchard

Gratitude

There are many people to particularly thank, all of whom in their different ways have been a source of considerable support over the past few years. They include Sue, Saphieh, Simon, Deborah, Keith, Catherine, Andrew, Sean, Charles, Brian, John, David, Martin, Neil and Sarah, who have offered such kind and outstanding care and counsel. Likewise, I must mention Mark, Deborah, Alan, Henrietta, Nigel, Henry, Jonathan, Robin, David, Angela, Jess, Judith, Ian, Stephen, Gareth, Tom, Simon, Katherine, Peter, Stephen, Iain, Morag, Robin, Sue, Jill, Mike, Martin, Andrew, Gilo, Paul, Terence, Christine, Michael, Prue, Howard, Tony, Anthony, Jane, Linda, Gill, Jill, Sue, Hilary, Alison, Ralph, Johnny, Dan, Peter, Nicola, Charles, Alan, Adrian, Dominic, Kim, Tina, Simon, Maggie and a host of others who have been truly dogged and determined friends throughout the past couple of years. The ever-redoubtable T@4 group has provided care, kindness and counsel ... with tea and cake. Likewise, the Monday Lunch and Prayer group has provided care and company. This group comprises around eight Oxford Heads of House who gather each week in term, and pray the liturgy of Sext taken from the *Cuddesdon Office Book* (1st edition 1858; new editions 1929, 1940, etc; Oxford University Press) and then over some lunch, talk through our issues of concern in a spirit of mutual encouragement. This group has existed for well over a century (though obviously the original membership has since moved on). The provision of other valuable support has come from my close family, and an even wider circle of friends I too often take for granted. Closer to home, the Cathedral staff, Chapter colleagues and College community here have been unstinting in sustaining and caring for us. Emma and I will both be forever grateful to each and every one. Last, but certainly not least, I record my gratitude for Emma for her love, fortitude and resilience. Our love and life still grows after more than 30 years of marriage. In turn, we continue to take delight in our wonderful sons, Ben and Joe, who both continue to provide us with their love, care, conviction and courage.

And special thanks to Alice Woudhuysen (1926–2020) for her lino-print pages iii and 177.

MWP, Epiphany 2021

A Personal Preface
(On Being a Bad Evangelical)

I begin with a confession, and one that will hardly surprise some readers. I am something of a dissenter. A loyal one, I dare to hope. But a dissenter, nonetheless. Or a 'reasonable radical' (Markham and Daniel, 2018), as others have put it. Socialism, pacifism and Quakerism are hard-wired into my Anglicanism. I cannot read the Scriptures without being prompted to ask questions about power, privilege and polity. Yet this spirit of dissent and protest has purpose: establishing peace and concord. But this can only be done when dominant uniformity is named and challenged, and individuals and communities permitted to explore their harmony and unity, and value their differences. So, if you have come in search of some pure pedigree theology, this book witnesses to something more hybrid. We can berth this approach within Anglicanism – a 'cross-bred' denomination if ever there was one.

Tracking my own trajectory in spirituality, theology and various causes in public life and the church I have been engaged in, there is some evidence of a pattern. To some extent, that same patterning is in this book, but it also flows from my vocation, which first stirred (startled and disrupted might be better words) when I was 16. And by the time I had turned 18, I had already had a couple of revelations. The first was that whatever career I might want for myself (indeed, I had several grand plans and other serious projects in mind), it was not to be. For by then, I already felt called to ordained ministry, and also to teaching. I cannot claim specific qualities in either. But can at least say I have tried to be obedient.

However, it is the second revelation that has taken me several decades to process. And it is this: I am a Bad Evangelical. Yes, Bad Evangelical. By which I mean what, exactly? Well, I am not a post-evangelical, of that I am sure. I have not moved beyond my roots. On the contrary. They are as strong as ever. Biblically grounded and orthodox, I believe in God as creator, sustaining and redeeming the world. I believe in Christ: the virgin birth, the purpose of Jesus' incarnation and death, his physical resurrection, his bodily ascension, and therefore his physical return. I believe in the Holy Spirit, the Giver of Life and Abundance who brooded over creation, and continues to comfort, counsel and confound us.

So, what is it that actually makes me a Bad Evangelical? Oddly, most of the things that, once upon a time, used to make Good Evangelicals. I believe that 'God so loved the world that he gave his only Son' (John 3.16). This isn't a conditional gift; nor is the love conditional. You might reject the gift and the utter, overwhelming and abundant love of God that sends it (note tense – it was, is, and will be, constant). So, you are loved by God before you are converted. Or if you never do turn to Christ. This is demonstrated in the life of Jesus, who humbled himself, even to the point of accepting death. Jesus chose to become one of us, in order that we might become one with him (Philippians 2).

This book was written at a time of enormous challenge and change in society, and so in the church too. Of course, every generation of Christians that have ever lived has lived in modern times, and every era of modernity presents challenge and change. Our mistake in the church is to presume the present moment is exceptional, when in fact the only thing that is constant is challenge and change. But the fear that accompanies the present can often evoke personal and collective reactions: fight, flight and fright, for example. The church, as the body of Christ, is more hormonal than it supposes, and the fears we face or imagine are often an acute response to stress. The purposes of the chapters in this book are intended to offer some realism combined with reassurance.

The former Bishop of Durham, Dr David Jenkins, was a

much-loved pastor and teacher, and often used to console congregations with these words, 'Don't worry about the Church of England not being up to it, because the good news is God is already down to it.' Jenkins belonged to that classic lineage of Anglican theologians whose ministry was rooted in the incarnation. The consequences of this for him – and many others like him – were spiritual, social and political. Perhaps more crucially, Jenkins' confidence lay in the gospel and the person of Jesus to whom it testified. He was an encourager, because he knew that God had chosen to dwell among us as one of us – and that needed living out in the coalmines of Durham as much as within our churches. Jesus' mandate of the Kingdom of God was not a private recipe for configuring congregations, but rather a vision for society in which Christians took a lead and shared responsibility.

Yet it is easy to be befuddled by the church, and become hexed by our complexity, and then mired in internal wrangling and stasis. Faced with this, many are tempted to lapse into despair and dread, unsure of what today (let alone tomorrow) will bring (Matt. 6.25–34). The church often lacks strategic patience, and is too keen to react rather than reflect. Yet even in the Gospels, Jesus offers enlightening perspective for today. There are things to fear, and fear often has an object, or a rational cause. In contrast, despair and dread usually lack an object, but they are paralysing, absorbing and distracting. It then becomes easy for the church to try and maintain, regulate and protect itself through fright, flight and fight. This then leads to the rapid erosion of humility, and the equally rapid arrival of hubris.

I don't mean by this that the church should 'keep calm and carry on', as the saying goes. To be clear, we do have crises in Christianity. Our churches face innumerable challenges. But many of these are of our own making. Some readers may be surprised that this book touches on old issues such as class, snobbery, ethnicity and identities. I am acutely aware that I write as an adoptee, and happily so. My personhood and spirituality is thoroughly rooted in being welcomed, incorporated and loved. We know that human groups and communities often bond through affinities of choice, and some that seem natural to them. The identity of such groups is often consolidated at the expense of those who are not members. Even when we don't mean to, boundaries and borders are defended, often at huge cost to outsiders.

We may not be able to avoid this natural tendency in group-think and practice. Yet we need to become more mindful of the calling of the church to be a new kind of community, and of Jesus' life and work, and his vision for the Kingdom of God, that shed boundaries, beginning with the incarnation. The Jesus we first meet in the Gospels is the risk-of-God in Christ; God among us, undefended. The crucifixion confirms that. The mandate of Jesus was radical, spiritual and political; but also vulnerable, humble and grounded. The Kingdom of God offers a model of kinship that allows us to belong to God by virtue of adoption – God's love, free and unconstrained, that seeks the transformation of the world. Christians are not called to make a new tribal group, but rather invited to participate in the making of an entirely transformed and redeemed world.

The trouble with today's church is that it has self-isolated. It has taken upon itself the task of quarantining and shielding, lest it become changed by the very world it is supposed to be embedded and incarnate in to transform the world. Donald Reeves' *Down to Earth: A New Vision for the Church* (1996) described the Church of England as being in 'self-inflicted exile'. (Yes, the church has got some form on social distancing, alas.) Typical of Reeves was his remarkable prescience, and calling the church to change, in order to become a more vigorous and relevant community in today's world. Reeves was critical of the then current trends and attitudes in the church, but he was able to advance imaginative, positive and radical ideas for its future, many of which were rooted in his critically framed prophetic pastoral approach to ministry. Reeves pleaded for the church to take a leap of imagination, and join hands with those working actively for a safer world for our children and future generations.

Yet the church frequently falls short of this calling, and collapses into tribalism and self-isolation. In Peter Selby's pres-

cient book *BeLonging: Challenge to A Tribal Church* (1991),
he discusses the new kinds of tribalism at work in the Church
of England. Some of this is an 'old boys' network' with tight-
knit boundaries. It does not exist with obvious bigotry, but
rather through coolly argued defences of the status quo. A
kind of club, it might now accept female members, but only
if they behave. The club does just enough to show it is adaptive and changing, and so ticks the right boxes, but otherwise
remains stubborn and recalcitrant. The tribal elders propagate
forms of nepotism which can be found in contested arenas
that seek to keep privilege in power. Ethnicity, gender, class
and sexuality can all play their part in the unconscious bias of
the tribe.

The very title of Selby's book is not a misspelling: it is a play
on a word. We don't belong to a club. We belong to a God who
adopts and loves freely. In turn, God calls all of the church to
'be longing' for the Kingdom of God to come, rather than for
the survival of a tribal church in the present. Selby calls the
church to awake from its slumber, and realize its identity as the
adopted people of a generous and free God, who prophetically
calls us to break borders that alienate and discriminate, and
overcome boundaries that inhibit the open and free acceptance
of God we find expressed in the life of Jesus.

If your spirituality and theology begins with these roots,
then various things will flow on from this, quite naturally.
The likelihood is that Christian faith is configured around that
central question, 'Who is Jesus Christ for us today?' And other
questions come thick and fast. How did Jesus see and act in
the world he came to inhabit, witness to, and seek to transform? What was his agenda in proclaiming the Kingdom of
God? Why did Jesus confound his critics by the ways he read
the Scriptures and applied them? Why was he both the bringer
of peace and yet also the disturber of peace (by which I mean,
that apathetic status quo where abdication of moral, social
and spiritual conscience reigns, and injustices justified through
this corpus we call 'religion', or that body we refer to as 'the
church', that place where evil flourishes, because good people
do nothing).

The Jesus I encounter in the Gospels doesn't seem be especially pro-religion or pro-hierarchy. He strikes me as rather radical. Sometimes, frankly, a bloody nuisance. Especially if you are trying to ply your trade in the temple and make an odd buck to get by, and Jesus just walks in with a whip, and in the mayhem that follows, is breaking up the point-of-sale display materials on various stalls, letting the pigeons and sparrows fly off in a panic, and throwing over all the counter-tops to the floor and scattering the petty cash and that day's takings freely across the precincts. (I bet the shopkeepers and market-traders called security back then, as they would do now.) Some may go further, and say Jesus was something of a revolutionary. He was clearly for the poor, marginalized, oppressed, stigmatized and demonized. And yet, his message, medium and ministry, despite the outburst, is rooted in the very being of God: love, love, love. Nothing but love.

I cannot claim to have done any more in this book other than to issue the reader with an invitation. It is this. If we start with who God is, we will always see the world differently, and therefore ourselves and our neighbours in a fresh light. We will act differently too. That will usually put religion in its place and allow God to resume God's place in our life, faith, and world. When that begins – what we do next with our Christian belief and practice – is likely to be less about propping up our struggling, cumbersome institutions, and much more about helping God usher in the Kingdom of God for others. It was that for which Jesus came: to show us that there is another way to live and behold the world. Being part of the living and loving God who invites us into that work of changing the world was the original invitation – or call – to the first disciples. It is still the same today.

Beginnings: Down to Earth

He has told you, O mortal, what is good;
and what does the LORD require of you
but to do justice, and to love kindness,
and to walk humbly with your God?
Micah 6.8

Humility is that low, sweet root from which all virtues flow.
Thomas Moore

Some decades ago, I was engaged in ordination training for the Church of England. I still am, of course. Our training never ends. Like conversion to Christianity, it is not a date marked in the past, but rather perpetual work-in-progress: for we never finish being converted. Ever. As part of my ordination training, I was despatched on placement to a remote rural parish, where one day I found myself being assessed on my skills leading a Bible Study. I recall a group of curious and engaged laity, trying to grapple with the text I had set them, and the discussion I was leading – at the same time as marking me for my effort and expertise, and also trying to find the whole exercise vaguely educational and devotional.

What I especially remember about the Bible Study was the passage I chose: John 13 – Jesus washing the feet of his disciples, in which he elects to serve them, and so humbles himself. And I asked individuals to talk about a time when they had humbled themselves. They told moving stories about service, costly sacrifice, and of putting others before themselves. As we edged round the room, we came to the vicar. But he had clearly missed the point of this exercise, and instead told a long story about a time when he had been humiliated. The room went silent, unable to process the vicar's story about his pride and self-worth somehow being devalued, and his perceived loss of status. After what seemed like an age to us all (except the vicar), the discussion moved on, and no one mentioned the elephant in the room.

The difference between humility and humiliation is obvious. It is one thing to humble yourself. It is another thing to be humiliated by others. Humility is something done *by* us for others. Humiliation is something done *to* us by others. So, when Paul, writing in Philippians 2, says, 'Jesus humbled himself', this is for others. When Jesus washes the feet of his disciples in John 13, this is for others. It is the ground of being from which his virtues and action will flow. Examples of his humility pepper the Gospels: having conversations on the level with people who his critics say should be beneath him, or any decent discerning teacher of the faith.

Yet this humility means Jesus will walk and talk with women who are alleged to be unclean, or unsavoury; or be fraternal and maternal with gentiles, the poor, the set-aside, the downtrodden. The decision of Jesus to 'humble himself' is one he takes, and that leads to the extraordinary consistency in his actions and teachings. It becomes the basis for his love to extend to all those around him, as he consistently refuses to count himself above others. He is among us a servant and born in our form and likeness. He often chides those who 'get above themselves', or look down on others – because of their faith, morality, or apparent status.

So, in one sense, Jesus is the 'Verb of God'.[1] Yes, the 'Word became flesh' (John 1); but as the Verb of God, Jesus 'does' God. Jesus is 'the body language of God', but more than that, is the actual expression of God – in words, deeds, actions, silences, walking, being – of what God is *doing*. By understanding Jesus as the Verb of God, I invite us to remember that our language is broken down into several different components. There are nouns, pronouns, verbs, adjectives, adverbs, conjunctions, prepositions and interjections. Jesus as the Verb of God expresses what God is doing. When we read the Scriptures, we often get hung up on the nouns (where is Jesus, who is he with?). We often encounter pronouns in the Gospels too. For example, we almost never learn the names of the people Jesus heals. They are just he or she, or described by their condition (lame, blind, leper, etc.). Sometimes the Gospels give us adjectives (poor, rich, etc.) that help us to colour in the narrative picture the writer gives us. We might get the hint of an adverb too ('she rose slowly' or 'he ran quickly', etc.).

Jesus, as the Verb of God, sees and acts beyond the dominant nouns and pronouns of his day. Because a verb is a word that describes actions or a state of being, we can learn to 'read' Jesus as he walks, talks, moves, speaks, is silent or angry; and yes, heals. As the Verb of God, Jesus is frequently an interjection. Sometimes, literally, he is God's exclamation mark(!) in a situation. His actions and words demand and command the attention of those in the script or the drama, and interrupt the flow of what went before, and what is to come.

Yet this is not a book about grammar. True, our worship is a 'grammar of ascent' in John Henry Newman's memorable phrase. But I do mean that all our worship is a response to the grammar and reality of God's descent: 'he lived among us ... full of grace and truth' (John 1.14). Christ's lowliness – the stooping and coming among us – is the Verb of God coming to us, raising us up – as though we were Lazarus (John 11). Or for that matter, as any one of the countless people Jesus bends down towards, kneels beside, scoops up, carries and raises up. Jesus' verbalizing of God means that in all manner of parables, actions and healings, he is saying to us what he says to an unnamed young girl, whom he took by the hand and said, '"Talitha cum" which means "Little girl, get up"' (Mark 5.41).

It is probably the case that two of earliest hymns we have in the New Testament are the ones cited by Paul in Philippians 2 and the Prologue in the Gospel of John. We do not know if they were ever accompanied by music, but they are still today forms of poetry more than prose, and in liturgies they are often printed as Canticles, giving them the same lyrical quality as many of the Psalms of David. What is especially intriguing about Philippians 2 and John's Prologue is the stress both place on the grounded humility of Jesus: coming to live among us as one of us and taking the form of a servant. It is the Bread of Life that is shared from here – Jesus, the Verb of God, becomes the Living Bread in whom all our hungers are satisfied. The nourishment that flows from participating in his body is a food like no other, and the goodness and growth it produces cannot be measured.

The Scriptures are full of food, feasting and eating. Parables from Jesus talk of heavenly banquets that are for sharing with the apparently undeserving. His actions give us moving accounts of shared meals, breaking bread with friends and miraculous provisions for thousands. The Old Testament gives us manna, blessed bread, honey, cakes, forbidden fruit, more miraculous provision for thirsty and hungry servants of the Lord. The New Testament tells of more banquets and meals, gives us the first formulated words for the Eucharist, and invites us to share the fruits of the Holy Spirit.

The common feast to which all are invited is scripted in the Kingdom of God. When we read the Scriptures, we see that the church is called to be incorporative in what it does. It is to be a church of multiplication, not division. We are to add to our invitation list, and not divide, ration, or silo. The church is called to be an adopting community that is free and uncon-strained, like God. In life there are almost no bad foods, only bad diets (Spector, 2020). This is true spiritually, as much as it is true for the feeding of our minds and bodies. Our sharing of God's love and the fruits of the Holy Spirit is not determined by caste or class; gender or generation; orientation or origin. In Christ, 'there is no longer Jew or Greek, there is no longer slave or free, there is no longer male and female; for all of you are one in Christ Jesus' (Gal. 3.28). As these lines from one of Frank Colquhoun's prayers put it:

Lord, the feast is yours, not ours.
It is to your table to which we come, to be your guests …
… to receive as from your hands the bread of life, the cup
  of salvation,
and so, to find refreshment, strength and peace …
(Colquhoun, 1996)

A Knowledge of Pie and a Pie of Knowledge

For the earliest churches, shared meals and feeding those who could not feed themselves extended from the very heart of the Eucharist. Just as Jesus, the Living Bread, is for all, so was the church to be a community that fed and nurtured the widows, orphans and those who could no longer care for themselves, or whom society (or religion) had discarded. Bethlehem, where Jesus was born, means 'the House of Bread' in Aramaic. So, from the crib to the last supper, to Emmaus, and to our altars today, the bread we share is *banal* – common food, symbolic of spiritual and inward nourishment, that binds us together as one equal body.

Common food and common eating is the hallmark of fellowship. When training for ordination, Emma and I spent a year on placement at Consett in County Durham. This once proud steel town had been decimated by the economic ravages of Thatcherism, and rates of unemployment were high, with the other accompanying indices of health: obesity, smoking and long-term depression. Yet working with the curate and community there was a source of endless, utter joy. The congregation and parish were terrific company and moving exemplars of resilience and hope.

It is the leaven of the communal suppers and lunches that Emma and I often recall, over 30 years on. For the menu was always the same: corned-beef pie. It was sometimes served cold, in 'slabs', or hot, with a side of boiled potatoes. We never quite got the hang of the recipe, but it was essentially corned-beef mashed with potato and filling an 'envelope' of shortcrust pastry. It is fair to say that as a meal, it was filling. Indeed, I sometimes wondered with the winds whipping off the moors, if the function of this food was partly ballast. The top layer of pastry was not latticed, and it came as it came, hot or cold.

The appreciation for this local Consett fare lay in its commonality. We all ate of one social meal, and it therefore bound us together, so there was no enmity or any kind of competition in the provision of food, of cooking skills, and so of class, taste or other particularities that might divide us. Corned-beef pie meant something: this is us – we share our social life, lot, and fellowship together. There is one body. One pie. Irrespective of education or occupation, or the lack of either or both, there was no room for any sneering snobbery when it came to food – what the sociologist David Morgan (2018) defined as 'a matter both of public disapproval and private enjoyment'. All partook of one meal.

Years later, when Emma became vicar of a parish in Sheffield (Holy Trinity Millhouses), the common meal for the congregation was meat and potato pie, and minted mushy peas. Again, you might think, more ballast than nutrition? Perhaps. But this common, repeated menu had a quasi-eucharistic function. This is how we expressed our life together socially, not just liturgically. Like bread and wine each day, each week, the common meal for social occasions expressed our unity and our equality. Pie was for sharing. Just as Swiss hamlets still remember and celebrate the community bread oven located in the centre of most hamlets or villages, with the loaves apportioned out as each person and household needed through the long winters. This work was regulated in each community by a 'Banal' – our word for 'common', but the Swiss term for the village council that looked after everyone, so fostering the common good.

The term 'pie' has a similar social history. For at least a thousand years, it has referred to a baked dish comprising a thick layer of pastry, filled with ingredients and seasoning. It was often a food of the poor, as being dry, it could be transported without expensive crockery, cut up and shared easily, and also stored for some time. The pasty is a variant on this: food for the day, for one person, often folded (as pasties are, and pizzas once were – and in places still are). The magpie bird derives its name from its alleged 'pie-like' proclivities – lots of things, this and that, brought together in a nest – a rather incoherent jumble of things that have been collected and put together, yet somehow work. Humble pie, unsurprisingly, is as old as pie, and originally referred to a recipe made of the normally discarded innards of deer and vegetables – the venison meat being richer, and for the rich.

Our word 'omble' or 'umble' is from the old French word

for the offal of deer, and over time, 'omble' or 'umble' have been conflated with 'humble'. It is no accident that the fictional furry creatures created by Elisabeth Beresford in her books, and subsequently recreated for television – Wombles – draw on this word. The Wombles live in burrows on Wimbledon Common, where they help the environment by collecting and creatively recycling rubbish; reusing the things that 'everyday folk leave behind', as 'The Wombling Song' by Mike Batt puts it.[2]

To 'womble' (verb) is to forage – to hunt around for the unseen, the hidden, neglected and discarded. Jesus himself was an advocate of this kind of foraging: 'When you give a luncheon or a dinner, do not invite your friends or brothers or relatives or rich neighbours, in case they may invite you in return, and you would be repaid. But when you give a banquet, invite the poor, the crippled, the lame, and the blind' (Luke 14.12–13). In other words, don't go picking the plump low-hanging fruit. Instead, go to the highways and byways, the edges of society and beyond – and as Jesus does, delve for those lost and cast aside by society and religion.

Likewise, a humble pie was something made out of what was left over – by which I mean what was no longer wanted, or had been discarded. The phrase has gone on to gain common usage, meaning that the person eating humble pie is down and out, facing humiliation and needing to beg for forgiveness, restoration, and apologize for their failures or mistakes. The conflation of a pie made from deer offal and our word 'humble' is entirely understandable. Humble pie for the church is a vocation, not a humiliation. It is to share our commonality with all humanity, not count ourselves above others; and to listen and learn, rather than presume to always teach and preach.

This is not an easy lesson, but we must surely know that we can only revitalize the church through recovering what it means to be the Body of Christ; being, like Jesus, the Verb of God: being a humble body, grounded and earthed; a servant community leaving behind our self-importance and self-regard. For this reason, I am quite taken that prison-slang for the chaplain – who have to be, arguably, the earthiest clergy of all – is 'pie', as in 'The Pie wants to see you, and is waiting in your cell.' Prison inmate slang can be hard to follow, and connections not obvious. So, in case you have not got there yet, 'pie-and-liquor' equals 'vicar', which means 'chaplain'. Clergy are humble pie for prisoners and warders alike (Aitken, 2005).

Our very notion of humility comes from roots meaning lowly, grounded, earthen and low-born. Burrows are below ground; it is hard to live lower. The humble person is lowly, modest, self-effacing, unpretentious, simple, unambitious, ordinary, gentle, modest, respectful, and looking out for others to serve. The humble person will set aside self-regard: nothing and no one will be above them. So, a god who chooses to become humble – even unto death, as Philippians 2 puts it – is a scandal to the mindset of 2,000 years ago. Jesus, among us, is as common as bread. A humble birth was not for the gods. But it was for our God, who in emptying himself, chose humility. So, the site of Jesus' birth in Bethlehem is a sheltered burrow, and the site of his grave in Jerusalem a burrowed-out rock.

Jesus comes among us humble and grounded. Broken bread and shared wine speak of commonality: an everyday Jesus; a Jesus for everybody; a Jesus-in-ordinary. God, in coming among us, and so commonly, knows what he is doing. Indeed, this is the genius of God's recipe at work here. We perhaps forget that the first recipes were not for cooking food, no matter how simple. They were, rather, the blend of ingredients that con-stituted medicine for the body. So, our earliest 'recipes', in the stricter, original sense of the word, were for healing: they were salve, for mending, soothing, curing.

Today, most people associate the term 'humble pie' with a catastrophic 'come down': the realization of humiliation after hubris. It is what the arrogant get, and perhaps deserve, when they get taken down a peg or two: 'Ah, they'll have to eat humble pie after that defeat'; or 'I think we will bake them a humble pie to eat, after that incredibly embarrassing display.' But there is a different and better way of seeing humble pie. Suppose we see it as part of the daily diet of the church, and the gathering of what the world discards or counts for noth-ing? Suppose we see the church as a body that actively seeks to listen to and learn from the world – the foolish, not just the wise? A church that operates as a receiver of wisdom, not merely a broadcaster of propaganda? Rather than a church, indeed, that behaves like a choosy magpie bird collecting, for example, strategies and tactics for growth and management from the secular world of corporate business (well, OK, if you must), but then is completely deaf to how those same corporate businesses promote equality, diversity, learning and development – and practise proper employment and human resources. In fact, they are practised so well by many of our top business corporations, the lessons rarely need to be preached. The church, in contrast, preaches what it does not practise. Instead of trying to constantly present a Church Triumphant, what about a vision for a receptive, learning, humble church?

Whatever your knowledge of pies might be like, you may also be aware of something termed the 'Pie of Knowledge'. Devised in 1992, the concept is an attempt to describe your own knowledge of things in relation to all the knowledge in the universe by making a pie chart, like a cake, and cutting it into sections. There are five slices in all. The first slice is made up of those things that you know you know (for example, how to make a really good pie). The second slice is larger, and comprises those things you know you don't know (for example, how to make a nuclear reactor work, or the names of the moons for Jupiter, etc.). The third slice contains things you did once know but have forgotten (for example, your first mobile phone number, or first computer password ... or perhaps your present one). The fourth slice is filled with those things you cannot possibly know unless you have experienced them (for example, what was it really like to live in Auschwitz in January 1945, or to know from a very early age that you are not attracted to the opposite sex, but to girls or boys just like yourself). The fifth and last slice is intriguing: these are the things you don't know you don't know. (I can't help you with examples here – but it is the largest slice of pie; indeed, it is probably 99 per cent of the whole pie.)

The church that I know – or rather the one I think I know – often makes the mistake of conflating its own identity and abilities with the God it worships. God is all-powerful, all-present and all-knowing: omnipotent, omnipresent, and omniscient. The church, however, is not. As a body, we often act as all-powerful (but this hex usually only works on die-hard attendees). As a body, we like to be everywhere and into everything (parishes, chaplaincies, politics, economics, ecology, and so on). This is good, because although it means the church is spread very thinly over a great deal of terrain and material, the comprehensiveness is at least an attempt to express something of God's total and complete care for all things. As a body, we tend to presume that we are all-knowing, and this is by far our most problematic dimension to wrestle with. Because, in truth, the church I have come to know actually knows very little. We have opinions on many matters, but our knowledge and direct experience of how the world works, and how people live, is extremely slight.

There are many reasons for this. We cannot know everything, and nor should we assume we can. Which is why a humble, grounded church that listens, and is receptive and adaptive, is the key to the church recovering its vocation, and revitalizing its mission. We do have a gospel to proclaim. But we have a world to listen to, and immerse ourselves in. As with the Jesus we follow, the Word becomes flesh and dwells among us, precisely so the knowledge and experience of humanity can be drawn into the life of divinity. Humility, for Jesus, meant that he was prepared to venture outside his own comfort zones, and discover faith and belief in people who did not follow his own Judaism. Jesus found faith in Gergesa and Samaria; in people who followed other faiths or may have followed none. But his mission – his own humble self-exposure to people and places outside his faith boundaries – was something he allowed to inform him, teach him, and change him. It transformed his mission, taking it from the parochial to the universal.

Here and Now

That was there and then, and this is here and now. At the
time of writing, and at the time of reading for many people,
the world has been slowly emerging from the chaos and fear
wrought upon us by Covid-19. The last major pandemic in
the world was a century ago, when the 'Spanish Flu' (as it was
called) claimed more lives than World War One that lasted
four years. The Covid-19 pandemic has been indiscriminate
with the lives claimed, and with those left orphaned. The shock
of large-scale loss was predicted by few, and yet for every
thousand deaths, there are hundreds of thousands impacted by
bereavement. There is no vaccine for grief.

Rather like Judith Kerr's *The Tiger Who Came to Tea*, grief
involves entertaining an intrusive, disruptive guest that settles
down for a lengthy stay. It helps itself to our time and energy,
distracts us when we are trying to concentrate on more important things, and stops us finishing even the most basic tasks. It
tends to be untidy. It messes us up on the inside. Tasks that
once took us no time at all now take for ever. Energy levels
drop. We are always tired; yet we cannot properly sleep.

Emma Percy's remarkable poem 'Breathe' invites us to contemplate what might be involved in our next steps. The world is
a restless place. Old and familiar ways of being are struggling.
Some of that struggle is against new and more threatening
forces at work in politics, society and religion, in class, race
and gender; in communities, technologies and ecologies. Some
of these confrontations are tense, even violent. There is a sense
of breathless, restless, viral change. The underlying irony is that
the Covid-19 virus causes people to gasp for breath – panting,
gulping and fighting for the very air that gives us life. Percy's
poem speaks into this, and out:

> Breathing is always good.
> Slow, Steady
> Pause
> Take time in responding

Calm, measured
Speak
Carefully choose the words
Truth, honesty
Anger needs to be tempered
For righteousness' sake
Indignation tested
For self-understanding
Courage found to stand your ground,
For words matter.
Some things need to be said
Some voices need to be heard
Some certainties need to be challenged,
So, breathe, pause, and speak.
(Emma Percy, 'Breathe' 2020).

Our reality is stark. So much has stopped – work, sport, enterprise, travel and entertainment – we find ourselves living in a kind of universal Lent. To emphasize this moment, public religious life ceased too. This enforced 'perpetual pause' has brought a halt to our frenetic pace of life and our breathless race to squeeze more and more out of each minute of every day. Indeed, the virus has replaced that breathlessness with another kind of gasping.

Might there be some signs of good emerging from this crisis? Adjusting to a different pace and finding some deep stillness can regenerate our core sense of purpose. A core no longer geared towards frenetic busyness, or self-fulfilment, can become more fulsome and self-aware. This can make us more mindful of others – especially those who continually live in perpetual states of exile or with all manner of serious social restrictions. We only understand the gift of our freedoms when we experience their loss. The simpler way of life that is currently forced upon us may actually help us become more discerning – refounding our purpose, communities, and society on the essentials rather than the merely expedient.

This is all about perspective; learning to see the difficulties of the here and now as part of a much bigger canvas. At times of concern and worry, some sage counsel by a much-loved Jewish preacher-cum-teacher is suggestive:

> Look at the birds of the air; they neither sow nor reap nor gather into barns, and yet your heavenly Father feeds them. Are you not of more value than they? And can any of you by worrying add a single hour to your span of life? And why do you worry about clothing? Consider the lilies of the field, how they grow; they neither toil nor spin, yet I tell you, even Solomon in all his glory was not clothed like one of these. But if God so clothes the grass of the field, which is alive today and tomorrow is thrown into the oven, will he not much more clothe you – you of little faith? (Matt. 6.26–30)

Jesus' exhortation to avoid worrying would have seemed as curious to his original audience as it might to us now. After all, a Galilean rabbi suggesting that a region dominated by an occupying army, where freedoms were restricted, and life and death hinged on fickle decisions made by unaccountable authorities, must have seemed like blind optimism to most. They had plagues too. Yet the Gospels record Jesus saying 'do not worry' or 'do not be afraid' over 70 times. Don't be afraid of the storm. Don't worry about lack of food or clothes. Don't worry about death. 'Do not be afraid … I am with you.'

What of faith and fear in a time like this? Our English word 'worry' was originally derived from the word *wyrgan*, meaning to 'strangle', and is of Germanic origin. In Middle English the verb gave rise to the meaning 'seize by the throat and tear', and later to our word 'harass', meaning 'to cause anxiety'. It is ironic that one aspect of Covid-19 is that it takes the breath away. It is, literally, a 'worrying' virus.

Jesus' summons is simple: consider the world around you; become attuned to the cycles of life in all their depletion and abundance. We are being bidden towards a more contemplative perspective. This is not a call to adopt some kind of supine passivity. It is just that there is little point in worrying about things we can't control. The birds of the air and lilies of the field are instructive. There is much we cannot control:

wisdom strips away our pride and hubris and invites us to rest in humility.

Humble Church

Humility is often grounded in knowing that you cannot know everything, and so are prepared to receive from and be taught by others. Instead of hoping you have all the answers, the humble person knows they are incomplete, and is unafraid of learning and responding authentically to new questions. The Word made flesh shows the way. Christ, in being all-loving and loving-to-all, is able to live within the constraints of humanity, because love itself is receptive. It is dialogue, not just mono-logue; it is reception, not just projection; it listens, learns and changes, and does not presume to hide behind the power of propaganda. Truth and love, when embodied, will find a home in humility, but not in hubris.

Paul tells us in 2 Corinthians 4.6 that the glory of God is revealed in the face of Jesus Christ. It is a telling image and insight. Our faces are communicative and receptive. They register pain and sorrow; joy and laughter; rage and compassion. Our faces, even when we choose not to speak, nonetheless say something. The face of Christ is one of recep-tive and communicative love; one that listens and learns, but also reveals the love of God, despite and no matter what is said or done to that face and body. This is the calling of the church too: humble, learning, living – but above all, loving.

This book is broken down into three parts, and with some suggestions for further reading and study, designed for groups, retreats, conferences and other fora. The three parts are: Culture and Change; Challenges and Church; and Christ and Christian-ity. Underpinning the book are some assumptions, not least of which is that the church is consumed with its own pride and reputation, and has (doubtless unintended) slipped into a kind of ecclesial narcissism. Some counter-propositions are explored. Namely, the church learning to listen before it pre-sumes to speak.

In practice, that means the church learning, through the careful cultivation and practices of humility, that it needs to spend more time in reception mode than it does in broadcast mode. The church learning that its own 'ecclesiocentrism' is a form of vanity and pride, and that if we don't stop the church becoming 'self-obsessed' with image, productivity and growth, we will lose far more than we can ever gain, and that the very being of the church is at stake here. That a vulnerable church, created and redeemed, and functioning and following in the footsteps of a humble Galilean preacher, is still of more interest and appeal to the world than a blandishment spoken by bishops and platitudes peddled by prelates. The book does not tarry for too long in arenas that are concerned with sexuality – or other 'hot potatoes' the church cannot seem to handle – while the rest of the world puzzles at our ineptitude. (Readers will be familiar with my writings and views on these and other issues, and will have their own minds on these subjects too.)

William Hubert Vanstone's remarkable book of pastoral and constructive theology has served as a template for this text. Vanstone's book was first published with the telling title, *Love's Endeavour, Love's Expense* (1977). He wrote of his ministry in a housing estate in the sixties and seventies, and of his search for a theology that would sustain the church in its grounded mission, and himself – his humanity – in his vocation. His discovery was the God who chose to be humble and vulnerable could teach the church to live and love better. Authentic love can have no guaranteed outcome, and this love of God is expressed in humble, risk-filled vulnerability of self-giving. Ultimately, the cross is God's reaching out and down to us, and in Jesus, reaching up to and through us, to unite humanity and divinity: love's endeavour, love's expense. Vanstone wrote a hymn ('Morning Story, Starlit Sky') to express this, much like the one that Paul cites in Philippians 2:

Morning glory, starlit sky,
soaring music, scholar's truth,
flight of swallows, autumn leaves,
memory's treasure, grace of youth:

Open are the gifts of God,
gifts of love to mind and sense;
hidden is love's agony,
love's endeavour, love's expense.

Love that gives, gives ever more,
gives with zeal, with eager hands,
spares not, keeps not, all outpours,
ventures all its all expends.

Drained is love in making full,
bound in setting others free,
poor in making many rich,
weak in giving power to be.

Therefore he who shows us God
helpless hangs upon the tree;
and the nails and crown of thorns
tell of what God's love must be.

Here is God: no monarch he,
throned in easy state to reign;
here is God, whose arms of love
aching, spent, the world sustain.
(William Hubert Vanstone, 1977)

This book is, in the end, about exploring what church could be if it was not self-consumed, self-serving and self-important. It is about recovering our identity and revitalizing our mission through drawing on Jesus 'who, though in the form of God, did not cling to equality, but humbled himself' (Phil. 2.6–7).

PART ONE

Culture and Change

Upside Down, Inside Out

Humility is really important because it keeps you fresh and new.
Steven Tyler

If it is true that 'there are no bad foods, only bad diets', then three obvious questions flow directly on from this sagacious proverb. First, does everyone have access to the right kinds of variety in food and diet? Second, does everyone have enough to eat? Third, do we recognize that differences between people may mean that diversity in diet needs affirmation? By this third question, I mean that some people cannot choose what they eat – either because it is unavailable, too expensive, or that their body might not be able to process and cope with such foods.

Food stories are important in understanding the Kingdom of God. Tim Spector's (2020) work has shown that most of what we know about diets is based on an 'average' person, and this social-scientific construction of the average is invariably a white, middle-class, middle-aged male. Notions of ideal fat, sugar, fibre, alcohol and calorie intake make assumptions based on a handful of models, that invariably ignore specifics of age, class, gender and ethnicity. As Caroline Criado Perez (2019) notes, the very idea of 'average' suggests more than a statistical 'norm', which is inherently divisive, as some will be above, and some below. And many other kinds of 'average' will in turn, be based on an ideal 'normal', which makes those who don't fit that mould abnormal.

That is why Jesus' teaching on growth and mission is so careful, if not mindful. Some seeds work in one kind of soil, but don't necessarily fare well in every kind of ground. To some are given grounds to toil in, in terms of mission, that are stony, hard and unyielding. To others, the ground is soft and fertile, and to others, the competition of weeds and the hunger of the birds means that all growth is quickly snatched away. Jesus' teaching on the ecology of the Kingdom of God was always an invitation to take part in levelling off the ground around us, and to take collective responsibility for those who have less, or perhaps nothing. God's provision is for sharing out with others, not hoarding to ourselves.

Our language for food is inherently politicized. The term 'food banks' is perhaps our best example at present. They do exceptional work, and have become a staple necessity in harsh and unforgiving economic times. Yet the word 'bank' borrows from the world of monetarism, and indeed, that very monetarism might be said to be partly responsible for the existence of food banks. Banks 'lend', but they do not give. So how do we talk about money, the love of which is one root cause of another person's poverty? Our language that shapes our thinking about money is so ancient and ingrained, we rarely think about it. How did we ever come to talk about 'owning shares', when sharing is not about ownership?

Money-talk is elemental, and if one, for example, follows the ancient assumption regarding the four elements that comprised the world, these are still metaphors we live by: earth, air, fire and water. Earth-metaphors give us words like bank, deposit, foundation and grounding. Air-metaphors offer oxygen and lungs (in the economy), headroom and room to breathe in budgets; and like air, money is everywhere. Fire-metaphors give us consumption, overheated (economy), inflation, fire-sale; and even today people speak of 'burning through money'. Water-metaphors give us assets that are frozen or liquidated; our confidence in an economy can suddenly evaporate; excessive money leaves some people awash in cash, while others drown in debt.

This makes 'Food bank' a rather ambivalent term. Those for whom money is secure will find the idea of a bank reassuring. It keeps money and investments secure, manages what you have and may even pay interest. For those in debt however, banks can be places of pain, regret and remorse, summoning memories of repossession, unaffordable loans and the stigma of losing control of one's finances. Food-aid and bank become intertwined, adding guilt to any stigma already there. Terms like 'larder', 'hub', 'store' and 'pantry' would convey something quite different to those in need, and to those donating or supporting.

So, if the church is to become fresh and new, and return to being the revitalized body it aches to be, where do we begin? Here, we need the courage to turn the church inside out and let it be turned upside down. Yes, it will shake us, and we must begin with ourselves. Yet it is in the adventure of following Jesus that we trust we learn to start with nothing but ourselves: no props, targets, goals, grand plans, well-intentioned ideas, or anything of the like. Begin with God. The fourteenth-century Sufi-Persian poet, Hafiz, in his short poem 'Zero' opines that 'zero is where the real fun starts ... there's too much counting everywhere else'. Elsewhere in one of his famous short prayers he says, 'I am a hole in a flute that the Christ's breath moves through – listen to this music.' Hafiz wrote playfully about lovers of God, and God's playful love of us. His poetry revels in delight, tenderness, cherishing, kindness and the familiarity of lovers exchanging their love for one another.

In beginning here, we may have to acknowledge that as instruments of God, we are not perfect: a cello with some missing strings; a piano out of tune; a saxophone missing some screws or keys. We are, as bodies, cracked instruments – all of us – but God uses the imperfect to perfect; the foolish and the broken to shame the wise and the strong. So, although the words Hafiz uses are hard to convey from the Persian, the poetry is kenotic in character – yielding and surrendering to the divine, and delighting in the superb surprise of being filled with God's ecstatic love for the world. God's total, overwhelming abundance. Richard Henry Tawney (1880–1962), the economic historian, social critic, Christian Socialist and important proponent of adult education, used to speak of the 'reckless divinity' of God that is ready to sweep away the intellectual ideas that hold us back. He talked of 'risk-taking sensibility' (Tawney and Seligman, 2017). He knew it was morally and socially reckless not to take risks. Often, that means not being frightened of losing what you have. Sometimes, therefore, it is best to start with nothing.

As a committed Anglican, and a no less committed Socialist, I find it exasperating that our church is self-absorbed with its self-preservation. Once-upon-a-time, I recall being asked at an interview panel for a senior post in the Church of England what I would do in that particular diocese 'to get more bums on pews'. I replied – perhaps too quickly – that the primary purpose of the church 'was to get bums off pews'. I could see my score card was marked down at this point. In a similar interview sometime later, we never talked about the region – its politics, economics, local challenges or needs – for the panel just wanted to know how the churches were to be filled again. The sense of anxiety and fear about not growing in numbers and members, but shrinking, overshadowed everything.

Could I help? This new panel asked. I replied that if we focused our energies and resources on addressing the alleged problem of the empty church, its eventual emptiness would be accomplished. The one thing that was almost bound to accelerate decline was to talk about growth. If the church is the first thing on our minds, you can guarantee it will be the last thing on everyone else's.

Jesus' proclamation of the Kingdom of God was not a promotion exercise for serving the needs of the church. Rather, the Kingdom of God promotes values and practices that are for all humanity, independent of faith. The Kingdom Jesus proclaimed and propagated went beyond the parochial Judaism of his day. It preached abundant mercy, love, justice, forgiveness, diversity, inclusion, reception and transformation. It did not fret about growing synagogue congregations, or spend days hunkering down in seminars trying to devise strategies for growth. The Kingdom lives out of its values – and these are values that followers will die for, as Jesus did.

This inverse prioritizing changes the agenda for the church in the twenty-first century. What are we going to do about climate change? Or the oppression and marginalization of people who flee as migrants and asylum seekers? Or the persecution of individuals and communities because of their ethnicity, sexuality or nationality? What does the Kingdom of God bring to our challenges in caring for the elderly and ageism, or inequality and the poor? The church needs a complete restart if it seeks to be revitalized. The question is not 'how can we get more people into church?' but rather, 'how can we get more people from church to love and serve the world, as Christ would have us do?' Instead of trying to refill the church, start from a different premise: that if we put God and the needs of the world before the church, the growth that many so desperately crave, plan for and try and resource may actually come. But if we put the needs of the church first, we shall continue to empty.

Preoccupied with Productivity?

The church in every age has faced fundamental challenges. Many would cite the challenge of secularization or consumerism in our time as one of the tougher trials the church has had to negotiate. I am less sure, however. But I do think there are two distinct challenges facing the church today. Or rather, it is one challenge or coin, but with two faces. The single-most challenge that the church faces today is that of distraction; and its two sides are mission and management. We appear to be preoccupied with both, and to such an extent that the identity of the Church of England now finds that its energies are consumed with perpetual drives towards efficiency and productivity.

Yet the church exists to glorify God and follow Jesus Christ. After which it may grow; or it may not. Its performance may improve too; or it may not. But it is imperative that faithfulness is always put before any search for success. Indeed, for most of the population of England, church-talk of mission and numbers tends to drive away far more people than it ever draws near. Evelyn Underhill, writing to Archbishop Lang on the eve of the 1930 Lambeth Conference, reminded him that the world was not especially hungry for what the church was immediately preoccupied with. Underhill put it sharply in her letter:

God is the interesting thing about religion, and people are hungry for God ... We ask the bishops ... to declare to the Church and especially its ministers, that the future of organized Christianity hinges not on the triumph of this or that type of churchman's theology or doctrine ... the Church wants not more consecrated philanthropists, but a disciplined priesthood of theocentric souls who shall be tools and channels of the Spirit of God.[3]

As any student of early church history will know, the beguiling attraction of the very first heresies and heterodoxies lay in their simplicity. They presented the most attractive solution to any immediate and apparently unsolvable problems. For the first generations of Christians, these usually lay in the sphere of doctrine and praxis. For us as a church today, the presenting problem appears to be declining numbers in our congregations. Ergo, an urgent emphasis on numerical church growth must be the answer. Right, surely? But wrong, actually. The first priority of the church is to follow Jesus Christ. This may be a costly calling, involving self-denial, depletion and death. Following Jesus may not lead us to any numerical growth. The first priority of the church is to love the Lord with all our heart, mind, soul and strength, and our neighbours as ourselves (Luke 10.27). There is no greater commandment. So, the numerical growth of the church cannot be a greater priority than the foundational mandate set before us by Jesus.

It was Karl Barth who observed that the true growth of the church is not to be thought of in extensive terms, but those that are intensive. He argued that the vertical (or intensive) growth of the church – in both height and depth in relation to God – does not necessarily lead to any extensive numerical growth. He added that 'we cannot, therefore, strive for vertical renewal merely to produce a wider audience'. Barth concluded that if the church and its mission were used only as a means of extensive growth, the inner life of the church loses its meaning and power: 'the church can be fulfilled only for its own sake, and then – unplanned and unarranged – it will bear its own fruits' (Barth, 1958, p. 648). That would seem to settle the matter.

Moreover, many parish clergy, and those working in all kinds of sector ministries, already know this to be true. The church does not exist to grow exponentially. Mission is deeper than that. The church exists to be the body of Christ.

The pastoral theologian Eugene Peterson once commented that the one thing he had learned in mission and ministry is how complex measurable growth can be. Peterson draws on the theologian, essayist, poet and farmer, Wendell Berry. Peterson says that under Berry's tutelage he has learned that 'parish work is every bit as physical as farm work: it is about these people, at this time, under these conditions' (Peterson, 1992; Bonzo and Stevens, 2008).

The pastoral turn towards an agrarian motif is arresting. Jesus told several parables about growth, and they are all striking for their simplicity and surprise. Especially the parable of the sower (Matthew 13.3–9). This parable should be the template for all Diocesan Mission Action Plans. For what Jesus is saying to the church is this: have regard for your neighbour's context and conditions. So, you might work in a parish with the richest soil, where every seed planted springs to life. The seasons are kind; the vegetation lush; the harvest plentiful. But some places are stony ground; and faithful mission and ministry in that field might be picking out the rocks for several generations. Others labour under conditions where the seeds are often destroyed before they can ever germinate. Or the weather is extreme in other places, and here we may find that although initial growth is quick, it seldom lasts.

The question the parable throws back to the church is this: what kind of growth can you expect from the ground and conditions you work with? And this is where our current unilateral emphasis on numerical church growth can be so demoralizing and disabling. Is it really the case that every leader of numerical church growth is a more spiritually faithful and technically gifted pastor than their less successful neighbour? The parable says 'no' to this. It implies that some churches labour in harsh conditions; some fairer. So be wise to the different contexts in which our individual and collective ministries take place.

I mention this for one obvious reason. If we continue to

place the heterodoxy of numerical growth at the heart of the church and its endeavour, we risk eroding our character, and our morale. Some will argue, no doubt, that if you aim at nothing, you'll hit it every time. Better to have a target and a plan than to just keep plodding on. But the Charge of the Light Brigade (1854) had vision, courage, objectives and some strategy; those were not in short supply. But the rest, as they say, is history.

Factors producing numerical church growth and decline are always complex. But the church might need to do some basic work on our maths. In the secular world, one plus one equals two. But counting and adding whole numbers in the church is fuzzy logic. Is a newly baptized infant 'one unit' in terms of believers? Does the person who comes every week, but has more doubt than faith count as 'one' or a 'half'? Is the regular, but not frequent churchgoer 'one' – or less? Is the person who comes to everything in church, but has a heart of stone, count as one? Or less?

We know that God counts generously. The poor, the lame, the sick, the sinners; all are promised a place at God's table in his Kingdom. That's why Jesus was seldom interested in quantity; the Kingdom is about small numbers and enriching quality. Yet we live in a culture that is obsessed by measuring things numerically and judging success from this. Fortunately, God is loving enough to tell us lots of counter cultural stories about numbers: going after one, and leaving the ninety-nine, for example, is reckless. Or dwelling on a single sparrow, or numbering the hairs left on your head – seemingly pointless.

God's maths is different to ours. And God does not easily concur with our cultural obsessions with 'growth-equals-success'. No one denies the urgency of mission, and for the church to address numerical growth. But the church does not exist to grow. It exists to glorify God and follow Jesus Christ. After which it may grow; or it may not. So, faithfulness must always be put before the search for success.

So, the key to understanding numerical church growth might be to engage in some deeper and more discerning readings of our contexts – the very soil we seek to nourish and bless, so the seeds can flourish. This will usually be more a complex piece of work than simply announcing another new vision or plan for mission. The pun is intended here: there is work to be done on the ground.

Topsy-Turvy

Christopher Hill's remarkable book, *The World Turned Upside Down: Radical Ideas During the English Revolution* (1972) reminds us that Britain endured a radical revolution on a par with the French Revolution over a century later (1789 onwards). My philosophy tutor was keen on engaging with Gerrard Winstanley, a largely self-taught theologian who was a mid-seventeenth century 'Leveller'. The Levellers were radicals: wanting to turn the world upside down, and their inspiration came from their readings of the Scriptures. They held that equality and community were fundamental for humanity, and that all hierarchies were a by-product of the Fall. So Winstanley wrote in his lengthy tract, *A Watch-Word to the City of London*, that 'true freedom lies in the community in spirit and community in the earthly treasury, and this is Christ, the true man-child spread abroad in the creation, restoring all things unto himself' (Winstanley, 1649).

Whatever you might think of Winstanley's proto-Christian-Marxism, and his radical advocacy of a kind of 'Cosmic Christ' now to be known in true (earthly) community spirit, his writings maintain their prescience. The English Revolution (known, wrongly in my view, as a 'Civil War'), was an era of clashing ideologies and a veritable melting pot of new ideas. All of this was born out of crisis. The old order was either gone or going. What would come to replace it? What was this brand new order going to look like?

We already know that crisis and opportunity are linked. For some, the opportunities in a crisis are simply ones that are ruthlessly exploited, and at the expense of others. But for many people, a crisis brings the best out of us, and causes lasting change. For example, were it not for the existential, social, pastoral and religious crisis of a young Church of England curate by the name of Chad Varah, there would be no Samaritans to call up when you – or those nearest and dearest to you, or more likely unknown to you – ring them in the small hours and pour out their sense of despair and isolation. Varah's crisis was a trigger for something creative.

What of now? I am not a big fan of movies that dwell on dystopias and apocalyptic scenarios that have been caused by some global cataclysm. Whether that is the third world war, malicious alien invasions, climatological catastrophe, zombies, Triffids (revenge of the neglected pot plants!) or just your ordinary class-generational-ethnic-nationalist-tribal-out-of-control-world competing for ever-sparser resources.

The premise that lies behind the dominant trope in this genre of movies is this: that faced with calamity, things will only get worse. Civilization will collapse; society will unravel; communities will disintegrate, and we will embrace 'every man/woman for themselves'. However, that is not what we are seeing in this global pandemic. We are witnessing what I would term as a profound 'supposition switch' and some serious 'theory turnaround'. The evidence for this is all around us. Take social distancing and self-isolation. One friend wrote to me the other day to say that they had never felt less alone right now, despite not seeing people. In the 'community' to which they usually belong – itself often marginalized and isolated by the (so-called) 'mainstream' – she reports that people were in touch every day and checking in on her. It has confounded her; but in a good way.

We have already begun to learn some new ways of living as a result of this pandemic. A truly charitable heart and a giving attitude is powerful and unstoppable when it is hitched up to serious social intelligence. Yet there is a crucial question within this observation: are you a claimer or a giver of opportunities? Most people think that life is all about 'taking your opportunities'. This is our conventional wisdom. But we live in unconventional times right now: the world is turned upside down. The new question is this: what opportunities can I now give to others? Including the 'others' I don't know. Yes, to paraphrase Donald Rumsfeld, the ones I know I don't know; but what about the ones I don't know I don't know?

Whatever way the world is turned, we are social animals. We were made for company. We need to develop a more cultivated wisdom now, that takes the veneer off our old conventional wisdom. Why do we say 'people live on benefits' when we all know we mean basic necessities? Even innocent terms such as 'Social Security' can be deceptive. Social Security usually only refers to a system of economic safety nets. It seldom does much to secure a person's value and sense of belonging in a community.

Our true social security lies with each other. This might be what Gerrard Winstanley had in mind. Put another way, the state does not replace the essential and fundamental need for community. Our communities are grass roots; the ground to which we belong, but also the space we share with neighbours, known and unknown. Our term 'topsy-turvy' comes from the medieval verb, tirve – meaning 'to turn or to topple over'. 'Topsy' was flipping the topsoil over, putting it deeper beneath the earth so it could nourish and replenish the ground above.

Deep nourishment in our communities? Yes. Community spirit connects us in ways that no state can ever compete with. Time then, to work out what and where our community is. And not to take our opportunities, but to work out how to give them away to others, so that all may participate, share in, and be transformed by what each of us can do for one another. Christ beckons us to do no less for our neighbours (Luke 10.25–37). Jesus gives us a choice. Would you rather have a good Samaritan on your side, or a prayerful Pharisee? Too many in the church like to offer prayers but then do nothing to help. We duck out of action, lest it be seen as too partial or political. Jesus' parable suggests we might be better off with a good person of integrity, virtue, truth and justice helping us, because God always acts through love, goodness and mercy. Simply put, be Samaritan.

Beginning and Ending with God

Samaritans are good people to be closing this chapter with. In Jesus' time they were despised by the supposedly thorough-bred Jewish teachers and leaders, who claimed both purity and pedigree. Samaritans were mixed blood and race, and said to follow a hybrid religion. The very idea of a Good Samaritan was either a joke or anathema to many scribes, Pharisees and Sadducees. Jesus did not subscribe to this worldview, however.

Like God, Jesus was essentially colour-blind. To him, all lives mattered, and the colour of skin, the creed followed and the country a person was from did little to determine value and rank in his eyes. Jesus looked on all with love – and that love was measured out abundantly and equally. His ministry was to be the Verb of God, and so his colour-blindness – analogical, not literal – was manifest in the indiscriminate ways in which he loved and cherished others.

We may think that the kind of prejudice that stigmatized Samaritans 2,000 years ago, or Jews 2,000 years later across Europe under Fascism and Nazism, is a thing of the past. But discrimination haunts our world today just as much. Our assumptions about Caucasian normalcy, for example, extend well beyond the realms of fashion and representation in public life. In medicine, for example, acral lentiginous melanoma – a cancer that is common among dark-skinned people – did not even get a mention in standard manuals of cancer diagnosis and therapy until towards the end of the twentieth century. The 13 sub-types that afflicted Caucasian skin colour had by then been in those same medical textbooks for close on a century. One can understand, therefore, the angst of movements such as Black Lives Matter, and the persistence in pressing for recognition that all breath, all skin, all life – all is precious to God, expressed beautifully by Oyin Olapido:

> Strip me of this accursed Black skin, I want to live in peace!
> I watched this video with emotions I can't describe.
> But, America why? England, why?

I watched this fully aware that I am Black, living in a
    White world.
I am Black, in a white college.
I am Black, in a white country.
I am Black – and to many I am wrong!
For this, I cannot breathe.
For how long will this injustice prevail?
Slavery, oppression, repression, murder ... genocide.
Does God ever curse the oppressors of His people?
Or, does He simply look away?
If this is the God of the Exodus, isn't it time he drowns
    Pharaoh?
Isn't it time he destroys Pharaoh's army of brutal oppressors?
If only for a moment, to allow me to take the breath of life.
But, nay – this white-washed, blue-eyed Jesus
appears to side with the oppressors – is He the oppressor!
They have changed the hew of his skin,
changed His hair and changed the colour of eyes.
He belongs to them, and they are His oppressors.
How can I believe when I cannot breathe?
I cry at the death of my people.
I weep beneath the weight of hopelessness
of being brown, labelled black, somehow – being born wrong.
Strip me please, strip this accursed melanin off of me;
for a chance to live in peace,
I'll willingly shed this skin,
for a chance to breathe.
But, I cannot breathe,
my life is like a wobbly, fluttering flame to be snuffed out.
I have no power, I cannot breathe;
I die daily at the hands of those who hold the guns,
who hold the power, who hold the wealth, who hold
    the Bible.
I cannot breathe, because I am Black,
this White man's knee remains ever constant on my neck,
blocking my airways, stifling my screams, ignoring my pleas,
I cannot breathe.
I cannot breathe, I cannot breathe.

God of my ancestors – where are you?
God of the heavens where are you?
As for this blue-eyed Jesus,
He and his comrades, they are silent,
And, their eyes have looked away.
I ... cannot ... breathe.
(Oladipo, 'I Cannot Breathe', 2020)

In his short but highly influential essay 'Created and Redeemed Sociality' Dan Hardy writes:

> The task of theology, then, is to begin from common practice and examine its quality in open trial by the use of natural reason in order to discover the truth of this practice, by a truth-directed reason ... (including) practical reason. And the outcome ... should be an agreement on the proper organization of common life which would actually promote the practice of society ... The concern is public ... the use of public reason, open trial of the truth and the achievement of truly social existence. (Hardy, 1989, p. 33)

We were reminded earlier of the implied ministry for the church contained in Paul's phrasing: 'the glory of God is revealed in the face of Jesus Christ', and that Jesus is the 'body language of God'. God occupies the world through Christ and in so doing becomes especially 'sensate' to its pains, sorrows and grief, as well as its joys. The churches are invited to be that body, with that same skin. Our churches are sacramental vocations: there to occupy and abide; and bridge the gap between created and redeemed sociality. The church is meant to hold and cherish the world before God. As the body of Christ, we are called to be nothing less than the social-sacramental skin for the world – for all the creeds, colours and communities we serve (Percy, 2017b).

A Plague of Numbers

Pride must die in you, or nothing of heaven can live in you.
Andrew Murray

On 15 August 1665, the weekly statistics on deaths in London were published. *Bills of Mortality* had been continuously published since 1603 by the Worshipful Company of Parish Clerks. By 1665 London had 130 parishes, and these *Bills of Mortality* provide a fascinating insight into how people viewed health, safety and mortality. On 15 August 1665 eight people died of 'excessive winde', one person from 'lethargie', one from being 'frighted' (more were recorded in previous weeks), another from 'meagrome', over 100 from 'teeth', just 15 from 'wormes', six from 'thrush' – and over 6,500 from something called 'plague'. The register adds that same week there were 168 Christenings.

London's plague of 1665–66 recorded almost 70,000 deaths, although the true figure is probably over 100,000. Charles II and his court left London during this pandemic and retreated to Oxford. (In fact, Charles II lived in the Deanery at Christ Church, as his father had done in the English Civil War – a conflict that spread virally to the rest of Britain and Ireland and claimed almost 15 per cent of the population over a ten-year period.) To say that the plague of London – the Great Plague, as it became known – was devastating, is to understate the matter. In just 18 months, almost a quarter of Londoners died from bubonic plague.

We have tended to view this tragic pandemic of seventeenth-century London through rather rose-tinted spectacles. Our present political leaders have, to a large extent, paid little attention to similarities in the dynamics that made London a no-go area in 1665–66, and during Covid-19. Frank Snowden's *Epidemics and Society: From the Black Death to the Present* highlights how the massive increase in urbanization and inter-continental travel has exposed us, globally, to new pandemics (Snowden, 2019). The warning signs were already here: HIV/AIDS, Avian flu, Zika, Sars, Ebola – to name but a few. We assumed that the teleology of our highly developed societies gave us immunities to recent afflictions, such as polio, tuberculosis and Spanish flu. In fact, some of these older diseases and pandemics – typhus, cholera, smallpox, consumption – have been surfacing again in the twenty-first century. Poverty and cramped, poor, unhealthy social conditions, act as breeding grounds for new viruses and bacteria. Malaria always thrives in environments where there is polluted, still water. It still kills five million children a year under the age of two.

In one recent letter to the editor of *The Economist* the author reflects on the way leaders responded to the Plague of Athens (430 BCE). The writer draws attention to the remarks of Thucydides regarding the behaviour of the leaders of Athens at the time who 'stopped at nothing in their struggles for ascendancy', caring little for the good of the state 'but making party caprice of the moment their only standard'.[4] In words that echo down the ages to the here and now, he adds that 'in this contest the blunter of wits were most successful'. So, Snowden argues that pandemics have always reordered society. They invariably result in a 'new normal' emerging. Out of the hysteria, superstition, tragedy and loss, comes a realism that reboots society. This can prompt fundamental political and social reordering – some good, and perhaps some not so welcome.

Our ancient forbears had a Latin phrase we would do well to remember: '*salus populi, suprema lex esto*' ('public health is the highest law, and all else follows from it'). So, the market-ization of health, welfare and other forms of basic care runs enormous risks for both developed and developing countries. Healthcare, rather like education, is an inherently not-for-profit enterprise. Why? Because everyone matters. And everyone eventually picks up the bill for the deprivation of education and healthcare in other places, because it will always directly or indirectly affect the whole of society. Politicians and people can try and evade their official and civic duties and responsibilities; but cannot avoid the consequences of such neglect. What we sow, we reap.

Snowden's book confirms what we know from other more popular studies of medieval England's health. Jack Hartnell (Hartnell, 2018), John Hatcher (Hatcher, 2008) and Ian Mortimer (Mortimer, 2009) all give interesting insights into how the plague-pandemic of the time reordered society – politically, financially and socially. For example, people born to serfdom might suddenly find that they were beneficiaries and heirs. Pandemics redistributed power and money; they challenged authorities and prevailing social constructions of reality; they promoted new consciousness, and reordered priorities.

The common denominator across these studies is that there is not much one can do to escape pandemics and their social and economic consequences. Plagues come and go. We are seldom ready for them. When confronted by their reality, we often go into denial. The numbers published on Covid-19 have as much impact as the *Bills of Mortality* in 1665. Most people say to themselves, as they have done in previous centuries, 'It won't happen to me.'

In the short, prescient 1947 novel *The Plague* or *La Peste* by Albert Camus (1991) we encounter a story that narrates a plague sweeping the French Algerian city of Oran. Initially, just a few die; then some more; then even more. Panic grips the streets as the epidemic enfolds the population. No one was ready for this, and few thought any plague could draw near to them. The citizens of Oran live in a state of perpetual denial. Even when, like London in 1665–66, a quarter of the city is dying, they reason it will not be them. These folks are, after all, living in modern times. They have newspapers, cars, aeroplanes and telephones. The people of Oran cannot, surely, perish like the poor wretches of seventeenth-century London or eighteenth-century Canton?

The hero of the book is Doctor Rieux, and his resilient humanism is profoundly moving. He does not buy into the religious interpretations of the plague offered by a local priest, or of the abrogation of reason by the citizenry. As the death-toll peaks at 500 per week, Doctor Rieux reflects on a child he has tended, but who has died. He reasons that suffering is unevenly and randomly distributed. For all the theodicy in the world, suffering simply makes no sense. It is absurd – and that is the kindest thing one can say of it.

How does Doctor Rieux respond to what is going on around him? He works tirelessly to lessen the suffering of those in his care. But he is no hero. As he later remarks that '[this] may seem a ridiculous idea, but the only way to fight the plague is with decency'. Another character enquires of him as to what decency is. '[Just] doing my job,' replies Doctor Rieux. In other words, duty and vocation come first. He is committed to caring for others in need. Little more need be said.

Should this, or any plague, panic us? Camus' novel suggests not, because panic is an immediate reflex response to a danger-ous, but essentially short-term condition from which we can flee and seek safety. But in life, there is no guaranteed security. From Camus, through Doctor Rieux, we learn the following lesson. That we need to love our fellow humans (whether we like them or not, no matter how long they live for, or how much time they take to die), and work with courage and hope for the relief of suffering. Life is ultimately a hospice, not a hospital. We are here to provide some salve in the midst of desolation and despair.

As the novel closes, Doctor Rieux opines that 'this chronicle could not be a story of definitive victory', because the plague never dies; it 'waits patiently in bedrooms, cellars, trunks, handkerchiefs and old papers' for the day when it will arise again. One might think this is a depressing note to end this novel on. Yet I do not think so. It is profoundly humanitarian. In selecting this adjective 'humanitarian', I choose the word with care. Because to be humanitarian is to have a binding duty and concern for helping to improve the welfare of people, and this pulse can spring from moral and religious roots. To be a humanitarian can be religious and humanist (and neither party will mind which), because it is about valuing people as inherently precious. Or as God would value them. The result is the same. It is the lesson of the good Samaritan (Luke 10). Or the ten lepers (Luke 17). Goodness for goodness' sake: not for gratitude. Or for converts. Mercy matters.

Correspondingly, there is nothing explicitly 'Christian' about Dame Cicely Saunders who founded the modern hospice movement. Committed to the alleviation of suffering, she wrote to her patients: 'You matter because you are you, and you matter to the end of your life ... we will do all we can not only to help you die peacefully, but also to *live* until you die.' Similarly, Chad Varah, a curate from Lincoln, founded the Samaritans to help the suicidal and the depressed. All it took was the suicide of a young teenage girl, traumatized by her commencing menstruation, to restart Varah's vocation.

Both these examples are profoundly humanitarian, and the religious pulses within them are lively, if implicit. Sometimes it is only the shock and despair at the manner of people's deaths that leads us to review the actual lives of others, and how to respond. Think Live Aid. Think Christian Aid. 'We believe in life *before* death.'

Like many people, I have been perplexed by the hijacking and hexing in the daily government briefings on Covid-19. Facts are true, and statistics are numbers you usually can't argue with. But presented in a disingenuous way, numbers and statistics can seriously mislead. There is one simple fact here: the figures for Covid-19-related casualties are stubbornly rooted in densely populated, poverty-challenged urban areas.

The real, underlying figures show that we are, as a nation, endemically unequal. Our epidemiologists find themselves unintentionally plagiarizing our social and political geographers mapping unemployment, disadvantage and other indices of poverty. Pandemics have patterns (that is, follow the money). As Albert Einstein once said: 'Not everything that counts can be counted; and not everything that can be counted, counts.'

So, I was deeply mistrustful of the rather specious government targets and numbers that were administered in daily dosage: 'two metres apart, no less'; '100,000 tests a day'; 'no, make that 250,000'; 'more beds, Personal Protection Equipment (PPE) and ventilators are on their way'; 'we are pumping another half-a-billion into our hospitals'; and 'more nurses are coming soon'. Throw in a weekly round of applause for the NHS too, providing some ritual substance. One suspects that the 'numbers theatre' from Downing Street at the time was to distract us from more troubling numbers. Deaths in care homes, for one. Other nations have struggled too: Brazil, Russia and the USA have seen similar issues with leadership, economic use and manipulation of their health and mortality statistics, and rather cavalier attitudes to public health and political accountability.

Einstein was right. For what can measure the loss of trust by so many, when it only concerns the actions of a few? We need to be mindful of what we count; and always question the value attributed to any numbers we are invited to note (and those we are asked to ignore). Everyone matters. No one is expendable. There has been no number or statistic in this pandemic that can be countenanced or justified. For all the talk of 'spikes', 'flattening curves' and 'keeping the number below R1', there have been over 100,000 preventable deaths at the time of writing. Which means at least a million preventable bereavements.

One of the most heart-rending BBC interviews I have seen was with a woman in New York City, who had lost her job. As have over 30 million other Americans. Like many who have found themselves unemployed, she lost her health insurance too. Most Americans have their health insurance tied to their employer. This woman was halfway through her cancer treatment and awaiting more chemotherapy. That is no longer possible, because she has no job, and personally cannot afford it. And even if she could buy healthcare, she would be bidding for slots that have already been block-booked and purchased by prioritized health insurers. She probably won't die of Covid-19, as she was living in perpetual self-isolation. As she remarked, testing for the virus is free in the USA. Treatment, however, is not. In time, she reflected, she was destined to become another number – but probably a statistic that won't be counted in the 2020/21 round of the pandemic.

In 2020 I took a funeral for a friend, whose mother had died in a care home. Our funeral followed the protocols of the time.

One son present, with his husband, the Funeral Director, and me. It was not the funeral he would have planned for his mother in any other circumstances. Many more could have come, and would have come, were it not for restrictions on travel and the demands of social distancing. Yet we commended her to God's gracious care and keeping, and I thought of the words of comfort Jesus offers: 'where two or three are gathered in my name, I am there among them' (Matt. 18.20). I thought of times when Jesus sat with the bereaved (Luke 8, John 11). I was reminded of these words from Thomas Lynch:

> I remember the priest I called to bury one of our town's indigents – a man without family or friends or finances. He, the grave-diggers, and I carried the casket to the grave. The priest incensed the body, blessed it with holy water, and read from the liturgy for twenty minutes, then sang In Paradisum – that gorgeous Latin for 'May the Angels Lead you into Paradise' – as we lowered the poor man's body into the ground ...
>
> When I asked him why he'd gone to such trouble, he said that these are the most important funerals – even if only God is watching – because it affirms the agreement between 'all God's children that we will witness and remember and take care of each other'. (Lynch, 2003; Lynch, 1998)

This vignette, as if we needed reminding, expresses something of Christ's own divine humanitarianism for those who were marginalized, isolated and needy. The life and ministry of Jesus teaches us that to God, each and every one is precious. The detail of caring matters. As Luke 12.7 has it, 'But even the hairs of your head are all counted. Do not be afraid; you are of more value than many sparrows.' Put another way, to God, no one is expendable. We all matter. We are asked to live as God sees this world: everyone matters.

Social distance between God and humanity is abolished in the incarnation. God is with us. We would be wise to remember that 'perfect love casts out fear' (1 John 4.18), yet also remember that the reverse is also true: 'perfect fear drives out love'. Our calling as Christ's followers is not to be fretful and fearful, but rather to become an extension of God's courageous, end-lessly expended love for this world.

This does require quiet mettle, resolved courage and com-passionate humanitarianism. As a calling, it is inherently costly and sacrificial in orientation. Such love does not seek its own security, or indeed reward. Our calling is to express the con-tinual love and risk revealed in the incarnation; to become like Jesus, who is the body language of God.

The philosopher John MacMurray wrote few books in his life, but one of his most absorbing meditations is on the essence of communion between individuals, groups and societies. We are all connected. In his *Persons in Relation*, he also noted that it was important to distinguish between real religion and fake faith (MacMurray, 1970). The mantra of the fake-variety, he argued, ran something like this: 'fear not; trust in God; and God will see that none of the things you dread will ever hap-pen to you'. But, said MacMurray, real religion has a different starting point: 'fear not – some of the things you are most frightened of may well happen to you; but they are nothing to be afraid of'. 'Do not be afraid,' says Jesus; 'do not fear'. Have courage, faith, love, hope and charity. It will be enough.

Harold Kushner's *When Bad Things Happen to Good People* sold millions of copies worldwide. But few recall that this best-selling book grew out of his own personal loss. Kushner was a rabbi who dedicated the book to the memory of his young son, Aaron, who died in his early teens from an incur-able genetic disease.

The book was written by a good man who prayed very, very hard – but who still lost his son. Like Doctor Rieux and Albert Camus, Kushner knew that real religion is not measured by how we avoid suffering and loss, but rather how we engage with it, and abide with and care for others who have lost even more:

> people who pray for courage, for strength to bear the un-bearable, for the grace to remember what they have, instead of what they have lost, very often find their prayers answered … [because] God … doesn't send us the problems … but God

does give us the strength to cope with them. (Kushner, 1981, pp. 125–7)

Loss may be the defining theme of 2020/21. People around us, and people we know, losing their jobs and livelihoods. If they have not lost them already. The distancing did not help us, either. Because it led to increased feelings of loneliness, and many of us already felt lonely. Only a matter of weeks before we could not have foreseen this. And we had only seen the beginning of the losses that were to come.

There is no upside to this, but as with most things in life that we face, there is a lesson. Naturally, it is not the kind of lesson that anyone can merely teach to someone else, as if it were a matter of having the right information. No, this is a lesson that must be absorbed. The lesson is that life, in the end, is partly about loss; and even suffering itself can be the teacher.

You may think this is a bit bleak. I don't think so. Many people experience significant suffering in their lives. Even our youngest citizens are already well-seasoned in this, and they show remarkable cheerful resilience and great humanity; maturity and fortitude beyond any reasonable expectation.

However, some suffering changes us forever. It creates, if you like, 'the new normal'. This can be the death of a parent or sibling, the pain and stigma of abuse, or the affliction of an illness. Most of us are spared these things. The loss we face in bereavement does not usually come until we are older.

But there is now a new normal – a pandemic where none are immune. It is likely that every one of us, in every community, will feel or witness this loss close up. In-built to the essence of life is the reality of losing it – nothing that lives can live forever. I know that might sound both fatalistic and a little pessimistic, but again, I don't think it is. Instead, it is honest and potentially freeing. But how so?

Being very partial to poetry, let me share Mary Oliver's short, pithy poem, 'The Uses of Sorrow':

Someone I loved once gave me
a box full of darkness.
It took me years to understand
that this, too, was a gift.
(Oliver, 2007)

We sometimes labour under the assumption that progress is inevitable, and things will only get better. Whatever is lost will be recouped. Others are under no such illusion. For progress is not inevitable – and not everything gets better.

For many of us, it starts inside us. We get older, slower, wiser, but less quick. Our friendships weather – but not always well. Parents get older and need our care; at precisely the same time some of us are raising children, who also need our care. We lose the luxury of being carefree. We lose free time.

That may sound a bit grim – even depressing – so how is it freeing? Like this. It is truly liberating if we can learn to accept that our lives are on loan, and that we are meant to share and give our lives over to others. That is the kind of lesson we are often taught when we are younger, though it often sits within us as a kind of 'noble idea' or even an optional virtue to toy with, depending on our mood.

But many of the things that mark us, or even scar us a little in adult life, show us that the idea of our life being on loan is a high, rich and rewarding outlook. It can govern our bodies and our relationships; our charity and love; our vocations and professions; our fears and hopes; what to receive, and what to give. One of Emma Percy's poems puts it like this:

I kneel in the pew
my soul is weary
there are knots in my heart and my mind;
anger, hurt, self-pity, self-blame.
We confess that we have sinned ...

Then the choir sings.
Treble voices soar effortlessly high
the other parts bring depth, breadth, harmony

and I am lifted.
Like practised fingers the music eases the knots.
Like scented oil the voices sooth my soul.
Kyrie, kyrie eleison.
And I am immersed in the possibility of mercy.
Caught up in the hope it offers
of forgiveness, of wholeness, of healing
Kyrie, kyrie eleison.
(Percy, 'Kyrie Eleison', 2020)

We have probably always known – at least notionally – that we are limited, fallible and imperfect. As much as we might be boundless, clever and good. But life is a teacher and reality a supporting tutor. To be human is to be vulnerable. To be a better human is to help others with their vulnerability and to be honest about our own. Right now, I'm figuring we all feel pretty vulnerable, or know we soon will. I know we cannot talk about this pandemic as some kind of 'gift', but there is an element of gift in this one fact: we are all, at the same time, being confronted with our individual and collective vulnerability. We cannot control it all.

Years ago, I remember reading the unsettling opening paragraphs in Alasdair MacIntyre's *Dependent Rational Animals*. Just now, his words seem prescient in a new way:

> We human beings are vulnerable to many kinds of affliction and most of us are at some time afflicted by serious ills. How we cope is only in small part up to us. It is most often to others that we owe our survival, let alone our flourishing, as we encounter bodily illness and injury, inadequate nutrition, mental defect and disturbance, and human aggression and neglect. This dependence on particular others for protection and sustenance is most obvious in early childhood and in old age. But between these first and last stages our lives are characteristically marked by longer or shorter periods of injury, illness, or other disablement, and some among us are disabled for their entire lives. (MacIntyre, 1999)

When the ill, the injured and the otherwise disabled are presented in the pages of moral philosophy books, you might be forgiven for thinking this is about others. But in truth we are all vulnerable, in some ways dis-abled, and of course dependent. At times, our dependency is not so pronounced, and so we see ourselves as the potentially benevolent moral agents – rational, capable, secure. Our assumed independence is forgetfulness about our dependence, and the false promises and hopes of our 'unending independence'.

The irony of adulthood is that it is precisely when we reach the point where it seems like our independence will have been maximized, we are reminded of our dependence – both from within our own bodies, and from the world around us. That is 'the gift' of this time, hard though this is to say. A truth is being told – we are all vulnerable and dependent, and far more is contingent than certain.

Life, I think, is not always about making the future we want, and creating entirely new worlds of possibility for ourselves. Sometimes it is about responding to loss and pain with virtue, charity and love – and facing the present and future with humility, integrity, truthfulness and courage.

In Thornton Wilder's *The Bridge of San Luis Rey*, we meet a Franciscan monk ruminating on the pointless deaths of five people who fell from a bridge. What is the point of this, he muses? Where is God's purpose in this tragedy? He writes in the Introduction that: 'some say we shall never know, and that to the gods we are like flies killed on a summer day, and some say, on the contrary, that the very sparrows do not lose a feather that has not been brushed away by the finger of God.' (Wilder, 1927, p. 176)

Wilder's novel is absorbed with values and virtues, and it offers a spiritual and humanitarian meditation of dwelling in the midst of senseless suffering. One character, Dona Maria, reflects on what it is that distracts people from the reality of pain and anguish:

[she] saw that the people of this world moved about in an armour of egotism, drunk with self-gazing, a-thirst for compliments, hearing little of what was said to them, unmoved by the accidents that befell their closest friends, in dread of all appeals that might interrupt their long communion with their own desires.

Yet Wilder ends his novel with an affirmation of what the Gospels ultimately assure us of; namely God's total care and love for everyone, wherever and whoever we are:

But soon we shall die and all memory of those five will have left the earth, and we ourselves shall be loved for a while and forgotten. But the love will have been enough; all those impulses of love return to the love that made them. Even memory is not necessary for love. There is a land of the living and a land of the dead and the bridge is love, the only survival, the only meaning.

We are plagued by all manner of numbers and statistics in our age. But even plague-related numbers and statistics may not be looking and counting in the right way any more. We are asked to see as God sees, count as God would count. One stray hair, one stray sparrow (Luke 12.7), one stray sheep (Luke 15.3–7): all matter. Each person is made in the image of God, and precious to God's sight and heart. What drove the humanitarian impulses of folk such as Doctor Rieux, or Cicely Saunders and Chad Varah – and many who currently work on the frontline of the NHS and in challenging social care contexts, whose names will never be known – is what Einstein hinted at. Everyone counts, equally. No numbers or statistics that any government promotes on pandemics, and that suggest it might be otherwise, have any real place in this world. Nor in the world that is yet to come.

New Era – From BC to AC

The greatest friend of truth is Time, her greatest enemy is
Prejudice, and her constant companion is Humility.
Charles Caleb Colton

It is too early to speculate on whether the government 'road
maps' for a post-Brexit Britain, and a post-pandemic UK will
be adequate. Time only moves forward, and we have certainly
arrived – unprepared, at speed – to a new epoch in our age. Our
twenty-first-century threshold has ushered in a new 'BC' and
'AC' – Before Coronavirus and After Coronavirus. Profound
and searching questions are yet to be asked of government,
services and institutions during our pandemic crisis. We have
found some familiar old heroes of comfort in this crisis. The
Queen emerged as the spiritual leader of the nation, with her
timely and sentient observation on 8 May 2020 (75th Anni-
versary of VE Day) that 'our streets are not empty, they are filled
with the love and the care that we have for each other'. Our
beloved, yet all too often beleaguered, NHS has been a shining
beacon of public duty, solidarity and sacrifice, supplying endless care and compassion, leadership and community service.

For all the talk of phases, however, there is no escaping the
recession phase that is to come. One in four citizens in the
USA will be unemployed. The UK economy is likely to shrink
by 15 per cent, and government borrowing will be at levels
not seen since World War Two. Our post-war era is losing
trust and confidence in the new faith of the developed world:
capitalism. The consumerist surges of the early 1950s, 1960s,
late 1970s and 1980s onwards created an unchecked culture of
aspiration that celebrated individualism and militated against
the communal. By upholding the sanctity of the individual (for

economically liberal, yet socially conservative ends – an odd combination), we slowly lost the communal.

Margaret Thatcher's political, moral and religious vision lacked a deep vision for social policy. Although widely misunderstood as saying, 'there is no such thing as society, only individuals', there was more than a grain of truth in this. True, it was arguably a headline for her politics, but not the real content. Yet what she actually said was this – and it is worth quoting in full – in an interview in *Women's Own* magazine, 31 October 1987:

> We've been through a period where too many people have been given to understand that if they have a problem, it's the government's job to cope with it. 'If I have a problem, I'll get a grant.' And 'I'm homeless, the government must house me.' [So] … they're casting their problem on society. And, you know, there is no such thing as society. There are individual men and women, and there are families. And no government can do anything except through people, and people must look to themselves first. It's our duty to look after ourselves and then, also, to look after our neighbour. People have got entitlements too much in mind, without the obligations. There's no such thing as entitlement, unless someone has first met an obligation.

I read these words back now in the light of the 'AC era' (After Coronavirus), and ask myself, 'what were we thinking of?' We've learned from Elizabeth Filby's recent study of Margaret Thatcher's religious outlook (Filby, 2015), that she sometimes struggled to comprehend the wider world. As her daughter Carol Thatcher once remarked, her mother would be exasperated that just as the financial markets in London were appearing to recover, they could be sent hurtling downwards as soon as the markets opened in the Far East. Carol once heard her mother say that 'this would all be sorted out if the whole world adopted Greenwich Mean Time!' To which Carol retorted, 'Mum, you have just condemned half the world to living in darkness.'

Our individualism of the post-war years created a culture of aspirants – ambitious, driven and focused. But nothing stands still, and it is often said that 'Thatcher's Children', in the end, grew to know what they wanted to *acquire* (property, cars, holidays, etc.), but not knowing what they wanted to *become* – and in relation to whom. Her vision was to create a country in the image of her father – an age of thrift, discipline and conservative values. It did not materialize. Instead, our present 'celebrity culture' offers more of an insight to what we have become. Gawping media-fuelled absorption with (so-called) 'personalities' who have considerable wealth and seem merely to pass the time indulging in conspicuous consumption. To be sure, these new 'heroes' of our age were not what Thatcher intended.

David Hare's play *The Power of Yes* (2009) gave us a gripping narrative of a dramatist seeking to understand the devastating financial crisis of 2007–08, which sounded the death-knell for over-hyped economic Thatcherism – the end game of deregulation in our banking systems and financial services. Hare constructs an imaginary conversation between a banker and someone working in public services. The character speaking puts it like this:

> People say, 'Oh get some private-sector people into the schools, that'll sort them out.' I doubt if there are many jobs in finance as hard as teaching a class of fourteen-year-old boys in a tough school. Because business is in some way quite simple, it has clearly defined aims. The aim is to make money. So, you have a measure against which to judge all the subsidiary actions which add up to the overall result. Managing a hospital is rather more complex. Because it's very hard to know what your objective is. There's no money-metric to help make the choice between better cancer care or having a better A&E. It's a judgement call. And running a hospital is an endless series of judgement calls where the criteria and objectives are very far from clear. So, don't tell me that's easier than making money.

Later on, another character says this:

> Once Bradford and Bingley became a bank, I remember taking an immediate dislike to a new non-exec who said, 'I want one thing from this company.' He said, 'What I want is regular, incremental growth.' In other words, he was saying 'This company must grow every year.' Now that we all know that nothing in the world shows regular incremental growth. You know that. I know that. (Hare, 2009)

Growth is no longer an axiomatic certainty. Capitalism, at least as we knew it, may not be the future. In our emerging era we will need different lenses for some fresh '20–20 vision'. Not everything can grow all the time. As Julie Burchill once remarked of Thatcher, it wasn't for pleasure or profit that she kicked away the crutches of the poor. Thatcher genuinely believed everyone *could* walk without them – and that the best way to help people was to take the crutches away. She was doing you a favour. As Norman Tebbitt famously suggested, once the crutches were gone, a bicycle could help. In the aftermath of the 1981 riots in Handsworth and Brixton, Tebbit responded to a suggestion that rioting was the natural reaction to unemployment: 'I grew up in the '30s with an unemployed father. He didn't riot. He got on his bike and looked for work, and he kept looking till he found it' (Ashmore, 2017).

The social challenges and changes that lie ahead are profound. The experience of riding a bike and some knowledge of the 1930s might turn out to be oddly prescient. That said, there has to be some serious engagement with what has and is happening to the world around us. In the UK, it is common knowledge that Covid-19 deaths had been drastically under-reported. In the first three months of lockdown, UK deaths attributed to Covid-19 stood at 33,000 – yet the 'excess deaths' up to 1 May 2020 were 55,000 – far more than the average for the previous three years. Approximately 40 per cent of those deaths were in care homes. No criticism of the carers is implied here, but serious questions must be asked about how to continue caring for the elderly and frail. There are over 120,000 care worker vacancies in the sector, and 80 per cent of care homes are run by private-for-profit companies.

In the first lockdown in the UK there was no guarantee that phases one, two and three of Covid-19 wouldn't continue to be entered and re-entered for some time. There was still a high probability of a return to phase one relatively soon. Covid-19 is so infectious that daily human behaviour had to be curtailed, simply to control the viral spread. Meanwhile, other problems have gone 'viral'. Mental health referrals have been at record levels. And the charity Refuge reported a 49 per cent increase in domestic violence.

We don't really think of plagues and pandemics today in the ways that our forebears did. But they were a common feature of everyday life for many centuries. Pepys wrote about them in his Diary. Shakespeare wrote *Macbeth* and *King Lear* while under plague lockdown quarantine. Not far from where I write – less than two miles east of Christ Church, at Cowley, is (St Bartholomew's) Bartlemas Chapel. Its adjacent Bartlemas Hospital was endowed by King Henry I back in 1126, so that the terrible threat of leprosy could be safely excluded from the city of Oxford.

Infectious diseases of all kinds were common enough in medieval Europe, but the twelfth and thirteenth centuries saw an unprecedented rise in leprosy right across Western Europe as crusading knights returning from the Holy Land brought newer and nastier threats to the public health of our island community. The public response was a mixture of pity and horror. For all that some wealthy and influential patrons tried to ensure a minimum of decent care for the sick, there were many others who went along with those primitive feelings of disgust and revulsion that led to a systematic rejection of the most vulnerable members of the community, who were ostracized to the very margins – way out in the fields, far beyond the city walls.

The church went along with this policy of exclusion. Literally following the injunctions of Leviticus 13, the church required anyone suspected of contracting leprosy to present themselves to a priest (with duly diligent social distance observed). If the leprosy was confirmed, the person was pronounced legally dead, cut off from society, and dispossessed of all their material wealth.

Christ Church archives detail a special ritual which accompanied this process of social banishment. It was presided over by the church in a chilling liturgy called the Mass of Separation. The unclean person was led out to the leprosarium after the fashion of a funeral procession. Typically, the victim was then formally clothed with a simple set of leper's garments, basic everyday utensils and a begging bowl. Sometimes they were actually forced to stand in a coffin for the duration of the rite. The priest then read out the binding admonition that would finally sever all links with the wider community:

I forbid you ever to enter a church, a monastery, a fair, a mill, a market or an assembly of people. I forbid you to leave your house unless dressed in your recognizable garb and also shod. I forbid you to wash your hands or to launder anything or to drink at any stream or fountain, unless using your own barrel or dipper. I forbid you to touch anything you buy or barter for, until it becomes your own.

I forbid you to enter any tavern; and if you wish for wine, whether you buy it or it is given to you, have it funnelled into your keg. I forbid you to share house with any woman but your wife. I command you, if accosted by anyone while travelling on a road, to set yourself down-wind of them before you answer.

I forbid you to enter any narrow passage, lest a passer-by bump into you. I forbid you, wherever you go, to touch the rim or the rope of a well without donning your gloves. I forbid you to touch any child or give them anything. I forbid you to drink or eat from any vessel but your own.

Our recent history teaches that fear, horror and primitive dread, in any society (whether ancient or modern, eastern or western) can provoke the cruellest reflex responses to fellow human beings who have the misfortune to represent some loathsome threat to the well-being of the community. Tainted.

Unclean. Excluded. Lepers. Then, as now, the identity politics that played out between powerful groupings in religion and society took a particularly cruel toll on some of the most vulnerable people. Lepers ejected to the margins were made to represent in their tainted identity the fears and forebodings of a whole community uneasy with itself. These were some of the ugly dynamics faced by Jesus in the healing ministry he offered, as he frequently touched the untouchable and the tainted, and drew the marginalized and demonized back into the social centre – then made them whole.

According to the World Health Organization, well over 90 per cent of the illnesses and diseases on this planet have a single cause: poverty. We lose five million children a year, under the age of two, to perfectly preventable malaria-related fever. Clean the nearby water supply and you eradicate the breeding grounds for the mosquitos that spread the disease. In the UK, obesity is now one of our biggest threats to health, and one of our biggest killers. Yet it is not a disease of the rich but of the poor. Maps of the United Kingdom spell out the demographics of obesity plainly. The concentrations of obesity lie in our poorest and most disadvantaged communities. A map of Scotland produced in September 2014 (Jeavens, 2014), showed that the concentrations of population voting 'yes' to Scottish independence correlated precisely with maps that chart concentrations of obesity (*BBC News*, 2008).

In turn, those maps of obesity also correlate pretty well precisely with indices of poverty and unemployment. And the maps charting the related consequences – cancers, heart conditions, and diabetes – follow in their wake. The areas in Scotland that voted 'no' to independence were, unsurprisingly, the wealthiest and healthiest. The map has too many similarities to the patterns of voting 'yes' for Brexit (*BBC News*, 2016). That map, in turn, looks very similar to the ones showing the 'concentrations' of Covid-19. Parts of London are featured. Towns and cities across the UK figure, and there is little escape for our deprived Urban Priority Areas; but you'll be fine in the wealthy shires.[5]

So, it does seem that there is a direct correlation between poverty, opportunity, housing, unemployment, education and health ... and finally, rates and ages of mortality, driven by underlying health conditions. Who knew? Our planet faces a bewildering number of crises at the dawn of the twenty-first century: global warming and climate change; pollution and a continued dependency on fossil fuels and minerals; deforest-ation and the degradation of our ecologies; migration and refugees; poverty and increasing inequality; congested cities and unsustainable living; ageing and declining populations in the global north with proliferating younger populations in the global south; unemployment; deteriorating levels of mental and physical health; and stubborn systemic issues in addressing collective social well-being. The list was already lengthy, even before factoring in the global pandemic.

We find ourselves in a strange season in difficult and demand-ing times. Covid-19 was not a moment in history any of us expected, nor a challenge any of us would have asked for. But it has been our time. A time tempered with a great deal of loss. How, then, shall we live? And how shall we respond? So, here is my advice: be truthful, be humble and be attentive.

Let me start with truth. It's more important than you think: truth it is not easy. It is about realism and honesty. It is not just about avoiding a lie, or spinning a phrase that misleads, but does not technically fib. Truth means this. Accept our losses as losses; but still find a way to give. I know that this might sound odd, and even completely counter-intuitive, because our basic instincts drive us towards recouping our losses. That is why the gift of this season is so strange and even alien. Our time invites us to recognize that we are vulnerable and dependent people. And in that, we may discover the powers of charity, consolation and cherishing. Our 'new normal' may build on the lesson of loss that suffering brings now, where we feel in a way we have not before: that each of us is ultimately depend-ent, and we are responsible for one another.

What of humility? Recent research from Harvard Business School – a famous study and essay, in fact from Jim Collins at the turn of the twenty-first century – found that many of the top organizations and institutions in the world were led by *humble* people. These were people that Collins identified as

'Level Five Leaders'; there are very few of them, and there is no higher level. They possess 'humility and fierce resolve', because humility is multi-dimensional and includes self-understanding, awareness, openness, passion and perspective. He continues, 'the most powerfully transformative executives possess a para-doxical mixture of personal humility and professional will. They are timid and ferocious. Shy and fearless. They are rare – and unstoppable' (Collins, 2001).

Collins never set out to study humble leaders. His study was the usual business school fare: how a good company might become great. But what he found was that these companies were developed by modest and wilful people, who had low ego needs, and could often come across as shy, peaceable and quiet. But they were also deeply resolved and highly resilient. They were not especially charismatic. They were more inclined to give praise to others and be quite self-effacing. Such leaders might say, 'it's not about me, it is about we'.

Their humility meant that they did not need much external validation. They tended to inspire with their concern for the small details of other people's lives. They tended to look only in the mirror for critical self-reflection, but otherwise looked out of windows. Leaders who were the opposite spent a lot of time in front of mirrors, and rarely glanced through the pro-verbial window. In this time of 'social distancing', now is the moment to be looking outwards and inwards, and asking, how can I help my neighbour, serve society and contribute to the common good? In a word, attend.

Now, attentiveness is not just sitting up and taking notice. It is a profound recentring of ourselves, and it requires us to pay detailed attention to that which others may not see or value. Attentiveness has an inner spirituality, fundamental to our humanity. Attentive love is rooted in humility: stooping to care for the small details and concerns of other people's lives *matters*.

Understanding that all lives matter paves the way for mutu-ality. That road is underpinned by the foundational rubble of humility. Consider this, for example. A tutorial question I sometimes used to set for undergraduates was to highlight the connections between Moses, the Buddha, Muhammad and Jesus. True, they are all great religious leaders. But there was also something stranger that connected them. They are all adopted. Moses was abandoned by his birth mother and left to float in a small coracle in the River Nile and had the good fortune to be picked up by the daughter of one of the pharaohs and nurtured as one of her own. Muhammad was orphaned at the age of six or earlier, and was brought up by his uncle in the ancient city of Makkah. The Buddha's mother died when he was less than a week old, and he was raised by her sister. Jesus, of course, according to Christian faith is not exactly the child of Joseph, since orthodox tradition claims no human intervention in his genesis. Although Mary is clearly his mother, Joseph is not his biological father. What Joseph needed to do was make space in his heart, mind and vision for a child that was not his; and to know that his role was to find space:

Mary needed room;
Room to be noisy.
To cry out in pain
To groan in labour
To curse the angel and her God.

Mary needed room;
Room to be messy
For waters to break
For blood, sweat and tears
For her body to follow its natural urges

Mary needed room
Room to be apart
Away from the noisy crowd
Away from the gaze of men
A place for women's work and women's wisdom

And in that room
In the noisy, messy, women's work of labour
A child is born

Hope is delivered
And the light came into the world.
(Percy, 'Room', 2019)

The founders of four of the great faiths of the world have something profound in common: their humility extended to dependency on others, and they begin their lives by being adoptees. In the same way, we too are asked to be less self-righteous, self-satisfied and self-sufficient – and become more self-aware. Notice what and who is around you. Notice who has helped you, even before you asked. Ask yourself who you can help, even without being asked. Don't expect to be thanked for any this, or even acknowledged. We are invited to humble ourselves and recognize our mutual dependencies. So, we are called to be kind, attentive, truthful, merciful and forgiving.

In our emerging AC era, we have to reckon with how we have allowed the largely beneficial 'viral spread' of capitalism to infect too many areas of society. If today's capitalism is now put under some closer scrutiny, we can see that for all the blessings it has brought, it is has also detrimentally commodified far too many features of existence and normal life that should be basic, essential human rights. To be sure, capitalism can, like a good virus, breed healthy competition within the body politic. Society becomes stronger as a result. But once the virus has freedom to move in spheres like education, health, social care and welfare, results are less wholesome. Our vulnerable warehoused elderly are paying an especially high price.

Ironically, the social distancing we're all now familiar with was already the experience of many who were cooped up in pockets of deprivation, exclusion and marginalization. The spread of Covid-19 has mirrored something of what capitalism had already done to us. C-19 is an unwelcome symptom of our obsession with individualism, unfettered growth, social mobility and inequality. As usual, the people who suffer the most have the least; they are more vulnerable and less mobile.

So, we have arrived at the inevitable 'WWJD' question: what would Jesus do? The question is only valid and useful if the church intends to copy the answer. And here it is. Jesus is the

Verb of God. He sees the unseen; hears the unheard; speaks for the mute and marginalized; touches the untouchable. The incarnation closed the gap between humanity and divinity. In Christ, there is no more social distance between God and the world.

It won't be easy to minister much longer by staying safe and at home. Witnessing through worship live-streamed from living rooms has been valuable and vital; but only one very small contribution in facing the challenges that lie ahead. This era is an *epoch* from which time is reckoned; we will learn to count our days *from* this moment. As we look forward, I hope and pray that we'll have the courage to be the hands, feet and voice of Christ in our communities once more.

There is a crucial difference between optimism and hope. Living in optimism has little capacity to deal with loss. But hope sees loss, damage and even death as something that has the ability to bring to birth new forms of life. Hope is the best of things, I think. We cannot live without hope. But hope has to be true and real. False hope is the worst of all worlds to be living in. True hope has courage. It knows that we are not complete, and that we need each other. It knows that hope is not just *what* we live for. It is *how* we live as humans – as individuals and as communities. We are asked to be, whether together or apart, scattered or gathered, constantly renewed: communities and persons of character and intentional virtue. Becoming this is all. Everything else is secondary.

There is a story about a rabbi who was asked to comment on the book of Genesis. The rabbi paused and noted that God had taken six days to make the heavens, the earth and all living creatures. After each act of creation, whether it was the light, land, oceans, plants, or any of the animals, God had pronounced them to be *good*. But on the sixth day, after God had created man and woman, the pronouncement of 'good' from God is conspicuously withheld. The rabbi cautioned his audience against concluding that humanity is not good. Instead, the rabbi noted that the term 'good' is actually a misleading translation of the original Hebrew word, *tov*. *Tov* simply means 'complete', 'finished' or 'sufficient'. And to complete his commentary, the rabbi added, you have to remember that humanity is not *tov*; we are still work in progress – incomplete.

Let us not forget that love, truth, attentiveness and humility all need to flourish in our world. We are the vessels for this. The call in this difficult and demanding time is to take off the frayed, light cloak of invulnerability and live together in truth, with humility and attentiveness towards one another. If our time now – with all the challenge that losses will surely bring – can lead to a future in which love and truth are stronger in us all, then this season will not have been in vain, and our time not wasted. The falling tears of our losses can become the seedlings of new gain.

PART TWO

Challenge and Church

Mind(ful) – the Generation Gap

Pride makes us artificial and humility makes us real.
Thomas Merton

Numbers may not give us an entirely accurate picture of what is happening in the world, but they can at least sketch the landscape we encounter. So, here are some numbers to help us locate the place of faith and religion in contemporary culture. In the USA, Generation Z (those born after 1985) are increasingly 'unaffiliated' to any religion: 36 per cent at the last count, and rising. Among those who self-identify from this generation as LGBTQ+, the figure is half as much again (around 55 per cent). In this same generation, only 22 per cent held their wedding in a religious house of worship in 2017 – down from 41 per cent in 2009. Around 70 per cent believe in some form of higher power, but only 20 per cent say they believe in the God of the Bible.

In case you think the picture emerging from this sketch is gloomy, think again, for something else is emerging. Around 30 per cent of Generation Z who self-identify as Christian also believe in reincarnation. New religions are on the rise, and its quasi-spiritual offshoots such as yoga, mindfulness and contemplative-health-spiritual-related exercises and retreats are booming. 'Enchantment', as Tara Isabella Burton observes in her sketchbook of contemporary spirituality and faith, is in our movie theatres and in our souls (Burton, 2020).

The word 'sketch', as a noun, derives from the Dutch s*chets*, the Italian *schizzo* (drawing), and the earlier Latin *schedia*, meaning a 'raft' or 'structure', and the Greek *skhedios*, that gives us the word 'scheme', and links to the English word 'schema', meaning 'shape, form and appearance'. To 'sketch' (verb) can also be to perform an outline plot or portrayal. A sketch is all I offer here: a rough drawing intended to serve as the basis for a finished picture. As such, it is preliminary, and claims nothing more. Its starting point is the following observation:

> After a relationship break up a few years ago, I signed on to a dating website. Filling in my online profile, I was interested to discover that the question on religious belief included an option that was new to me. You could tick boxes for the major religions, or for atheist, or for SBNR, which I discovered stands for 'Spiritual-But-Not-Religious' … One in three Americans defined themselves as spiritual but not religious. Millions of people now think of themselves as on their own personal spiritual path, but not affiliated to any specific religion. American sociologists Robert Putnam and David Campbell talk about 'nones' – people who belong to no religion but still believe in God. Others have used the term 'moralistic therapeutic deism' to refer to how young people are turning towards a vague belief that God exists and the point of life is to be happy. (Shakespeare, 2014)

Rooted in some earlier explorations (Percy, 2000; Percy, 2001; Percy, 2003; Percy and Ward, 2014), my sketch explores some aspects of the paradigm shifts taking place in religious affiliation for Millennials (also known as Generation Y) and Generation Z. For our purposes here, Generation Z (henceforth 'Z-ers') is one of several terms used to describe post-millennial youth born after 1996. Millennials are the generational demographic cohort following Generation X (those born in the 1960s up to the early 1980s). Together with Z-ers they present some interesting new dynamics to the study of religion and spirituality in the twenty-first century (Carrette and King, 2005; Heelas, 2005; Gortner, 2013). Iqbal writes of their social habits:

> So, what is the new 'going out'? Is the Generation Z idea of fun inexplicable to older adults? [My Generation Z interviewees] instantly refer me to Snapchat, where they communicate in

a constant group feed with their friends. Broadcasting the minutiae of (a) day – a good outfit, a trip to Westfield – is second nature. (Iqbal, 2018, pp.18–19)

The sketch I present here indicates, as will be especially apparent in the conclusion, that there are now strong forces and factors at work shaping Christian and other spiritual beliefs and practices, and through which we can identify a shifting landscape. (For a comparable 'narrative sketch' of a changing 'religious landscape', see McGrath, 1995.) According to Iqbal, Z-ers may prefer juice bars to pub crawls, and rank quality family time ahead of sex; and possibly prioritize good grades before friendship. As Iqbal notes, Z-ers are more likely to document their lives through Instagram and Snapchat – creating an audience for their lives who are immediately interacting. Somehow, sharing the image of a plate of food with a hundred other 'friends' is a 'social connection', helping to combat alienation, and engendering a form of socialization.

Observations

As the head of an Oxford college, I will make a few further points at this juncture. It is commonplace for many of my colleagues to assume that Z-ers lack emotional and mental resilience. There is anecdotal evidence for this view. A neighbouring college recently flagged a new 'resilience initiative' for its undergraduates and encouraged all new students to attend. But the older undergraduate body responded with criticism, saying they were 'hurt by the implication that they lacked resilience.' Yet, while this might seem to be the case on the surface – Z-ers are less emotionally tough, and seemingly more easily hurt – I hold that the picture is a little more subtle.

Z-ers are more sensitive on balance, than previous generations (Myers and Scanzoni, 2005; Gortner, 2013; Dean, 2010). In practice, this means that they are less inclined to discrimination of any kind, and broadly committed to equality – gender, sexuality, ethnicity and any 'protected characteristic' (for example, disability) – being taken as read. It is rare to hear an undergraduate making a joke that could be construed as sexist or racist, for example. But such humour was commonplace in my childhood – as even the seemingly innocuous 'there was an Irishman, Scotsman, Welshman, Englishman ...' jokes testified. One is just as likely to be censured for the sexism of such jokes today, as much for the 'man' reference as for the stereotyping of cultures and nations. Z-ers will be, in Kenda Creasy Dean's terminology, (almost incurably) 'nice'; and with that, almost Christian (but not quite).

What I also notice in undergraduates is a shift from the dispositional to the episodic. That is to say, they do not identify closely with, or become members of, institutions, groups, political parties, churches, or other organizations. They may join movements – but these tend to be 'seasonal' or limited to specific issues. They may join a gym but this is contractual, and it does not usually require anything other than the exercise of their consumerist assent (Carrette and King, 2005; Fuller, 2001; Flory and Miller, 2000; Gortner, 2013; Dean, 2010).

The concept of long-term membership of a group, institution or organization has become more attenuated for Z-ers. They are less likely to join a political party or trade union. But they may join a movement like Momentum.[6] Their engagement with value-based institutions will be occasional and consumerist rather than unequivocally committed. In ecclesial terms, joining a vogue-ish and niche 'Fresh Expression'[7] for a season is more likely to appeal than life-long membership of a denomination or congregation. Gratifying personal spiritual experience will come before collective duty towards or affiliation within an institution (Sargeant, 2000; Heelas, 2005; Jamieson, 2002).

Somehow, to borrow the sociological trope of Grace Davie (Davie, 1994; Davie, 2013) 'believing without belonging' has attained a new podium among Z-ers. They tend to be spiritual, but not religious (Gortner, 2013; Dean, 2010). And when they do turn up for any religious event or service, agreement or solidarity with the underpinning ethos or beliefs should not be taken at face value. Numbers do not mean what they used to any more. A hundred undergraduates attending a moody, sentient candlelit compline service in the college chapel tells us little about the condition of their souls, or the state of belief of any of the attendees, if those numbers ever did, of course.

There are not precise dates for when the Millennials' cohort started (or ended), but demographers and researchers typically use the early 1980s, 1990s and 2000s as guides to the birth years (Howe and Strauss, 2000). That places Millennials today in the 15–35 age range, meaning that the youngest Millennials have no memory of a time preceding the advent of social media, or indeed of the events of 11 September 2001. But defining generations is a little like dating centuries. Arguably, the twentieth century (in Britain at least) begins with the death of Queen Victoria in 1901, and similarly the twenty-first century is ushered in with the iconic attacks on the Twin Towers and Washington DC.

Nonetheless, I am cautious about terms such as 'baby boomers', referring usually to those born between 1946 and 1964. In popular mass-market sociology, this is the generation that invented free love, benefited from free university education, robust economic growth, and a prosperous jobs market. Generation X (born approximately 1965–81) benefited from a surge in late capitalism and the beginnings of a mass–market technological shift; but not yet computerized. Millennials (born approximately 1982–95), have many of the benefits of social media, but are also keenly aware that the previous two generations dismantled the concept of free university education, relatively accessible prospects of home ownership, and jobs for life. And finally, Z-ers seem to have the ability to hold a conversation and simultaneously scroll through their phones. They are globally connected and politically anxious. They are kinder, nicer and more sensitive than their forebears. But they may also be less resilient. They are certainly more 'fluid' and less 'binary', and more likely to experiment with gender and sexual spectrums.

Sketching Millennials and Generation Z

Our cultural landscape in the West is an unusual one to comprehend. Our world is not one of secularism or secularization. The twenty-first century is turning out to be a stubbornly religious one, in which absorption with anything from spirituality through to fundamentalism is seldom far from the news. However, we appear to have moved from a culture of assumption to one of consumption – with religion now a choice. As Dean notes, we are witnessing the rise of the 'nones': no longer atheists or agnostics; or Church of England by default; or Jewish because their parents were (Dean, 2010). Millennials, when asked what religion they follow, typically tick 'none'.

According to the Pew Research Center, formal attachment to religious organizations in the USA is in decline, and 'no affiliation' increasingly reported (Pew Research Center, 2014). Similarly, 'nones' now comprise a significant percentage of the UK population (perhaps up to third); and over 75 per cent of under 25s. But – and this is a big 'but' – many 'nones' do profess to believe in God. Yet they freely confess to doing little about it. The shifting cultural landscape is therefore this: Personal, Therapeutic Moralistic Deism is on the rise (Dean, 2010; Gortner, 2013; Center, 2014). The emerging generation is kind, considerate, tolerant and good. It will not stand for racism, sexism, homophobia or xenophobia. The emerging generation believes in many good things, and also in God (a bit, at least): but does not join a faith-organization to express this.

I offer some asides by way of comment here, as both an academic and a clergyperson. I am personally not much worried about the reduction in numbers where Christianity is concerned. History and sociology teach us that such things ebb and flow. I am far more concerned about the qualitative factor: what kind of Christianity are we talking about? It is not so much that Christianity is being secularized. Rather, more subtly, Christianity is mutating into a much broader, but also 'thinner' version of itself. Another way of labelling 'moralistic deism' is to say we are seeing the rise of the 'Almost Christian', as Dean (pp. 25–44) notes; being religious is being replaced by being nice. This might explain why, on a visit to a school some years ago, I noted the school's core values: no bullying; respect for all; recycle everything. One cannot quibble with this. But these values are not exactly the pillars of western civilization. They are not the Ten Commandments.

Into this equation, comes the sketching of an emerging generation. Until the early twentieth century, you were either a child or an adult; and there was no real sense of a transitional period of 'becoming' in between, unless you were among the privileged few who could afford the moratorium offered by travel or formal education. Adolescence is an invention or consequence of the late Industrial Revolution; a social pattern devised to keep young workers out of the factories so as not to displace older employees. By the twentieth century, thanks largely to access to public education, the 'moratorium' associated with adolescence had become widespread. The resulting age-stratification of society (which allowed advertisers to target youth as a 'market') created the crucible in which the 'teenager' – a post-Second World War youth with free time and disposable income – was born.

Today, adolescence continues to be a moving target. Puberty starts sooner and adulthood starts later; fertility and adolescence no longer go hand in hand. Scholars now posit emerging adulthood as a youthful life stage of its own, since the developmental tasks once associated with identity exploration (and therefore with adolescence) are increasingly postponed. Most young people eschew the title of 'adult' until their late twenties or early thirties. We seem to have learned to accept 21 as the 'new 16'. Today, adolescence functions as a lifestyle as well as a life stage, a state of consciousness as well as a period of life that young people can and often do prolong, with the full cooperation of contemporary culture.

The changes taking place in late twentieth-century religion have been charted by Roof (Roof and Greer, 1993) who focused on the baby-boomers, and on the impact on American mainline churches (Roof and McKinney, 1987). Putnam's *Bowling Alone* noted the collapse of voluntary institutions and neighbourly connections, with implied implications for religious patterns of belonging (Putnam, 2000). Putnam's more recent *Our Kids* charts the alarming acceleration of individualism in American society, which in turn lays the foundation for less corporate religion and belief, and greater emphasis on personal spirituality (Putnam, 2015). The landscape, then, is changing fast. Churches and other religious congregations are like marooned islets in an ever rising globally warmed sea of individualism and personal spirituality. The 'we' generation has morphed, arguably, into 'generation me' (Saliba, 1999; Gortner, 2013; Dean, 2010).

Thus, and according to Dean (2010, pp. 3–24) today's teenagers tend to view God as either a butler or a therapist, someone who meets their needs when summoned ('a cosmic lifeguard', as one youth minister put it) or who listens nonjudgmentally and helps youth feel good about themselves ('kind of like my guidance counsellor', according to one student). Most young people (even non-religious ones) believe that religion has much to offer, and those who attend church tend to feel positively about their congregations, even when they are critical of religion in general. Many teenagers say that religion benefits individuals or society, or both. The bad news for churches, arguably, is the reason teenagers are not hostile towards religion: they just seem not to care about it very much. Religion is not a big deal to them. The vast majority of US teenagers tend to be quite inarticulate about the faith, religious beliefs and practices that they have, and the meaning or place it may have in their lives.

In a telling analogy, Dean argues that religion has moved from being a matter of bounded, propositional, or behavioural 'territory', in which people locate themselves as 'in' or 'out', or 'on the fence'. Instead, faith has become something more akin to the proverbial African farm – one in which the landscape is vast and boundless. In other words, there is no fence at all. The only question to ask therefore is this: are you moving closer to the farmhouse, or further away? This is a kind of detachment from formal obligations, and the logical outworking of a religious ecology that is consumption-based, not assumption-grounded (pp. 157–84).

This is new landscape. But what is the ground of its being? Dean argues that 'niceness' is the new faith; and because there is little in the way of antidote to niceness, 'nones' are growing in number, across the generations. That said, 'nones' do value religion as being personally useful: in addition to helping people be nicer and feel better about themselves, religion can provide comfort amid turmoil, and support for decisions that (by and large) teenagers want to make anyway. Otherwise explicit and propositional faith stays in the background. Moralistic Therapeutic Deism has little to do with an immanent God or a sense of a divine mission in the world. It offers comfort, bolsters self-esteem, helps solve problems, and lubricates interpersonal relationships by encouraging people to do good, feel good, and keep God at arm's length. It is a kind of self-emolliating spirituality; its thrust is personal happiness and helping people treat each other nicely.

Sketching the Future

I suspect that the litmus test for assessing the extent of generational change and its implications for mission can probably be best understood by speculating about death and memorialization in the future. If our cultural commentators – who speak of 'Gospel amnesia' and 'a thoroughgoing fragmentation in lineage of Christian memory' – are right, then what will a funeral visit by a clergyperson look like in 2050? Until fairly recently, many Christian ministers conducting funerals could have been reasonably confident that, unless otherwise requested, there would be hymns and prayers at the ceremony. The Lord's Prayer might be said; some hymns – many learned at school – might be sung, and certain passages of Scripture and collects might be included and familiar to a number of the mourners.

But what of the future, where prayers, collects and hymns are not likely to have been part of their schooling for the vast majority of mourners? What types of religious sentiment will be uttered by the generation that is, in all probability, non-conversant in the language of formal religion, but fluent in the many dialects of spirituality? To partly answer my own question, I turn to an analogy drawn from the world of art history (Percy, 2003). Restorers of paintings sometimes talk about the 'pentimento': that is, the original sketch that is underneath an oil painting beginning to show through as the painting ages. The pentimento is a kind of skeletal plan (the first lines drawn on canvas): where paint falls or peels off, the earliest ideas for the picture are sometimes revealed.

The 'pentimento' analogy allows us to pose a question: what will the spiritual pentimento of Millennial and Z-ers' children look like when it comes to their funeral? It will, I suspect, at least at a church funeral, be primarily Christian, provided we understand the term 'Christian' broadly. It may be a kind of vernacular, operant (rather than formal), folk Christianity, not that dissimilar from what many ministers already encounter. But it may also be a more spirituality open and evocative affair, with readings from other traditions. It will also be more therapeutic in inclination, centred less on grief and more on celebration.

Recent research led by Margaret Holloway at the University of Hull, UK, has identified a marked shift in funerals and memorialization.[8] The approach to death in the UK is changing fast. Religious funerals are perceived to be inflexible, impersonal and overly formal. There is a growing trend for funerals and memorial services to be flexible, life-affirming (if not actually life-celebrating), bespoke, inclusive and hybrid in character. Funerals and memorial services can draw on resources that are rooted in religious traditions; but the practice of an entire funeral being an approved expression of that religious tradition seems to be in decline. There is ample anecdotal evidence of traditional memorials rapidly giving way to, and now coexisting with, a developing range of alternative forms of remembering the deceased. Moreover, the bereaved are choosing to use public spaces quite differently as they memorialize the departed – including founding charities, on-line memorials, or sharing meaningful rituals in significant open spaces (beach, woodland, hilltop), as well as marking deaths at park benches, roadside shrines and other places.

Some 20 years ago, in an article for the *Harvard Business Review*, Gilmore and Pine suggested that the 'experience economy' would emerge as a key cultural change in the new millennium (Gilmore and Pine, 1998). By this, the authors pointed towards new patterns of spending among Millennials. The emerging generation would focus less on quantity and more on quality; less on material acquisition and more on personal attainment. In practical terms, this means less spending on consumer goods, and more spending on lifestyle: eating, entertainment and 'experiences'. 'Experience', Gilmore and Pine argued, would become a distinct economic reality, and have its own power, and it would incorporate yoga, gym, travel – and religion (Gilmore and Pine, 1998).

This is in no way a critical remark, but I suspect that the stress on 'experience' is one of the overwhelming cultural changes to be seen in the twenty-first century. And 'experience' is essentially a celebration of life. It turns an individual mourning into a moment of personal loss to be reflected upon, individualized, and then shared on social media. Indeed, such change is arguably already upon us. Increasingly, ministers find themselves under soft socio-cultural pressure to provide a ceremony that celebrates the life of the deceased person and does not major on the actual mourning and loss that death brings. I presided at one such quite recently, and a mourner on leaving remarked that none of tributes had mentioned the fact that the individual we were remembering and mourning had in fact died. In fact, were it not for my own address and use of traditional prayers and scriptural sentences, death would not have been mentioned at all.

Equally, I recall attending a recent funeral for a young mother who had tragically died giving birth to her third child, leaving behind two children under five, and a husband barely 30 years of age. While this may still be relatively commonplace in the developing world and would not have been entirely strange to most Britons barely a century ago, advances in healthcare make such occurrences extremely rare today. At the crematorium, we celebrated the mother's life. And a symbolic centrepiece of the funeral was the coffin: not simply bearing the body of the young mother – but beautifully, hauntingly and some-what incongruously painted and decorated with the favourite animated cartoon characters that she and her children had enjoyed when watching TV together. The coffin had become a kind of toy chest; the type of furniture one might covet for a nursery. The funeral was presided over by a Humanist minister, who began the celebration of the mother's life with an affirmation that all faiths were equal and valuable, and that those who had come to the crematorium with no kind of faith were equally welcome. Nothing was void; equality of experience was assumed. Bright colours were worn by mourners, and the importance of this being a positive day to experience and remember was stressed.

Humans are a social, meaning-making species. Faced with death, birth and rites of passage, religion and spirituality still have their futures. And in all likelihood, the funeral of the future will be able to tell us just how much change has passed between our generations. And a pentimento of the present suggests an emerging future picture. I suspect that the religious-spiritual landscape we are now plotting has less content and more feeling. It will have far fewer propositions, and more per-formative relationality. It will leave memorable experiences, but far less to remember by rote. It will be less prohibitive, and more permissive.

Funerals, for the foreseeable future, will be broader moments of shared memorialization and experience. Shared on social media, mediated through multi-media, they will be more spiritual and less religious – but, I suspect, less alienating and more empowering for mourners. There will inevitably be gaps in knowledge and memory; but becoming generations have always found a way through to the past. There is no reason to suppose that Millennials and Generation Z-ers will lack the wisdom and the tenacity to do likewise.

As Hervieu-Léger (2000) points out, religion is a chain of memory. Stretched, and perhaps in some places, threadbare and even broken, it is a chain, nonetheless. After all, the original etymology of religion comes from two Latin words, meaning 'to bind together'; past and the present; individual and community;

heaven and earth; ordinary and divine. More sketching of this fast-changing socio-spiritual-religious generational landscape is still to be done.

Conclusion

Over 30 years ago, Roof and Mckinney noted that the transition among the emerging generation was now marked by a movement from formal religious observance and membership to 'surfing' from congregation to congregation; and by the emerging generation not belonging strongly to any one particular body of believers, but with an increased appetite for spirituality. They note that:

> Large numbers of young, well-educated middle-class youth[s] ... defected from the churches in the late sixties and seventies ... Some joined new religious movements, others sought personal enlightenment through various spiritual therapies and disciplines, but most simply 'dropped out' of organized religion altogether ... [there was a] tendency toward highly individualized [religion] ... greater personal fulfilment and the quest for the ideal self ... religion [became] 'privatized' or more anchored to the personal realms. (Roof and McKinney, 1987)

Collins has also pointed out that religion is merely *mutating* into significant forms of personal spirituality, rather than disappearing:

> Spirituality ... has moved from the self-spirituality of the boomer generation to a more aesthetic spirituality, a spirituality which is focused on pleasure and experience in and of itself ... Successful churches, it seems, offer an atmosphere and intimate experience of God over and above doctrine ... the spirituality of intimacy of the millennial generation will be deeply bound up with the consumerism that has increasingly concerned youth throughout the post-war period. (Collins, 2000, p. 183)

The added power of consumerism at the present time reinforces this sense: niche marketing to almost every age group for every stage of life is not only prevalent, but also highly successful. Roof notes that 'in times of social upheaval and cultural discontinuity especially, generations tend to become more sharply set off from one another' (p. 3). And in the emerging faith of Millennials and Generation Z, although desires appear to be still clustered around spiritual fulfilment and 'personal experience', there is also a craving for 'the authentic'. As Parks notes, there is a 'hunger for authenticity, for correspondence between one's outer and inner lives ... a desire to break through into a more spacious and nourishing conception of the common life we all share.' (Parks, 2011, p. 47).

I suspect that, increasingly, we shall see Millennials and Z-ers treating religion as an issue – albeit an important one – but mindful of the perceived pathologies of religious belief and practice (fundamentalism, discrimination, violence, etc.). With religion seen as a repository for problematic beliefs and practices, the field is clear for individualist spirituality to become ascendant. My sketch of this emerging, shifting landscape, then, appears to be pointing towards the foregrounding of personal experience and spiritual fulfilment, and suggests that formal and traditional religion is consigned further into the background. At present, it is hard to see a different picture emerging. But then, even 50 years ago, few would have predicted a sketch of such a landscape at all. The mandate for churches could hardly be clearer: listen and learn. Let go of pride, which is artificial, and strive to recover the grounded authenticity that has been lost. Humility makes us real.

Abuse, Authority and Authenticity

Real genius is nothing else but the supernatural virtue of
humility in the domain of thought.
Simone Weil

'Survivors' Protest aided by Chapter'

Two survivors of clerical abuse have praised the Dean and
Chapter of Christ Church, Oxford, for facilitating their protest at the consecration of the Bishop of Oxford last Friday ...
the two handed out leaflets to those attending the consecration. At one point, they were brought a plate of sandwiches.

'Some of the people who went past were embarrassed and
dismissive; but others made a beeline for us, and wanted to
engage. Several thanked us for being there. Of the bishops,
three or four came and engaged with us for as long as they
could,' Joe said ...

The Dean, the Very Revd Professor Martyn Percy, had
invited the pair back to Oxford to discuss issues surrounding safeguarding and the reporting of abuse, Joe said. He
went on: 'So it was not only a very effective protest ... but
was graciously received, and managed to create potential for
good dialogue.' (Wyatt, 2016)

I do, in all seriousness, wonder why this was ever reported in a
newspaper. Why? Because we showed hospitality to strangers,
which the gospel asks us to do. It seemed clear to me that,
for protesters who had travelled many, many miles at their
own expense, and would not have time to get lunch, or not
know where to go for any food, the obvious and good thing
to do was to share our lunch with them – to break bread with
them. To check on their dietary requirements, of course; and

to ensure there was even a bowl of water for the dog they had brought with them. The tiny details matter.

Cynics may say that this protest was killed with kindness. That our engagement was a PR-bluff. But the gospel commands us to care for our sisters and brothers – all humanity – with hospitality and generosity. Without motivation of personal or corporate gain. We are just commanded to do it. Because God loves them; and God loves a cheerful giver. So, engage, talk, listen; and give.

I completely understand why it might be tempting to handle this incident with the protesters in a different way. Legal counsel might say it is unwise to meet with or engage with the demonstrators, lest this open further opportunity for misunderstanding. Others may say it invalidates insurance policies. Other may say that this risks the communications and PR strategy: suppose the encounter turns ugly, and the media captures it?

But when I read the parable of the good Samaritan, I do not encounter the following. The Samaritan fretting about his own personal accident and travel insurance by voluntarily taking on the liability of a stranger in distress. Or of his bank intervening, to say that they will not underwrite the cost of the hostel expenses that the stranger might run up, as he has not been pre-vetted as a signatory on the Samaritan's account. Or the Samaritan, even for a second, wondering if the half-dead stranger he picks up at the roadside is part of an elaborate ruse or hoax designed to fleece the unwary of their possessions.

Nor do I read of my namesake, St Martin, pausing – as he cuts his cloak in two to give half to a beggar who is cold and starving, to reflect on how his personal possessions accidental damage waiver clause might now be invalid. He just cuts his cloak in two. Like the Samaritan, it is a pure and instinctual outpouring of compassion. It crosses boundaries. These gestures take deliberate risks. Yet they are hardly reckless acts. But they do expose one human to another human's vulnerability and need. But that is the gospel, isn't it?

I do understand today why we might be risk-averse, and value diligence, responsibility and prudent policies faced with the possibility of reputational damage and corporate jeopardy.

I understand the need for managers to help us assess such risks, to enable efficient systems, good communications and public relations. I understand the need for child-protection policies.

When Jesus teaches us about discipleship, he talks about risk; but he does not take the risk away. He warns us that we might die for this faith. He means this literally, not figuratively or metaphorically. We are to wash one another's feet too. No training is provided for this. We don't risk-assess the feet in advance before they come into our hands.

Child Sexual Abuse and the Churches

The Australian 'Royal Commission into Institutional Responses to Child Sexual Abuse' was clearly a very thorough, deep and wide-ranging investigation. It is finely attuned to the profound pain of the victims (Atkinson et al., 2017). This kind of work now has an international dimension too. The recent 'Independent Inquiry into Child Sexual Abuse in the Church of England' has considered the case study of the Diocese of Chichester (IICSA, 2019). Reports on Bishop Peter Ball (Gibb, 2017) and Bishop George Bell, in which Lord Carlile conducted an inquiry into a profoundly flawed investigative processes run by the Church of England (Carlile, 2017), have all highlighted major problems with the churches trying to police themselves. So, to begin, I would like to make three preliminary observations, before moving on to some more specific discussion – from the perspective of pastoral theology – and as this relates to all the churches as they currently try and address the phenomenon of child sexual abuse.

First, the striking thing, as always, is the inability of the church to listen; to see; to feel. But the Royal Commission has listened; it has seen; it has felt. It has noticed those things that were hiding in plain sight for years. It names them. It calls them out. In that sense, the Royal Commission's work is properly prescient and prophetic.

Second, the Royal Commission challenged the institutional narcolepsy that has beset the churches and covered up sexual abuse over many decades and generations. The findings are already a wake-up call: a siren – and a prescient pointer towards a future shaped by transparency and accountability.

Third, the work of the Royal Commission is practical. It is an exercise in applied ethics. It does not leave the future to chance. It knows that no future is risk-free. But futures, and freedoms, are about mitigating risk, and that through remembering – recollecting – we have the serious prospect of redemption. Forgetfulness is the enemy of justice. Good remembrance is the friend of the future.

As someone who sometimes writes and teaches in the spheres of pastoral theology, I think that one of the most serious problems the churches have in relation to child sexual abuse is continuing to 'silence subjectivity'. The victims of abuse frequently complain that the churches do not really *listen* to the experiences of abused people at all. They did not tune in to the pain, tears, betrayal and humanity of the abused. The pride, prejudice and hubris of the churches dominates; they fail to listen with attentive, silent humility. So, the phenomenon of child sexual abuse becomes another platform – institutional projective identification – for the bishops to tell us how tormented *they* feel and invite us all to participate in and re-experience their own agonizing. Having a semi-conscious sense of their own impotence, they then needed to hand this on. This impotence and torment was then projected on to the very groups they were supposed be listening to deeply, and giving support and justice to.

What could pastoral theology do here? A way forward is to tease out the differences between empathy, sympathy, and compassion. And here I draw on the work of Nel Noddings (Noddings, 1984; Noddings, 2002). Empathy, simply put, is registering that the person you are listening and attending to may have some similar feelings or experiences to your own. So here, you could say, 'I recognize this in you, because I recognize it in myself.' In that regard, for example, any 'empathy' for a bereaved woman who has lost her child will be something of a sham, unless the listener really has had a similar bereavement. If they have not, they cannot empathize. The whole notion of 'shared conversations' needs to at least grasp this basic point.

You can only empathize with a person who has shared at least part of your experience. What do the bishops know of abuse, and the way it leads to illness, mental health issues, alienation, shaming, marginalization and oppression? Not much, I am guessing.

Then there is sympathy. The concept of sympathy is richer, and contains the sense that feeling is something that can be truly shared. The word comes from the Greek: *syn*, meaning 'together', and *pathos* which means 'feeling'; hence the idea of 'fellow-feeling'. But those in power will deny their own feelings, project them on to others, and then pathologize them. Sympathy, deeply rooted in any pastoral dialogue, will be a real and rich exploration of 'all desires known ... no secrets hidden'. It will be risky stuff, with all parties making themselves profoundly vulnerable, each to the other. The lack of sympathy, and indeed the near total 'empathy deficit' from church leaders towards victims of abuse, is notable.

Then finally, there is compassion. This is, of course, what God in Christ has for all creation. The incarnation and cross represent the pre-eminent passion; it is the fullest demonstration of God's *com*-passion for humanity. Compassion is what motivates people to go out of their way to aid others who carry physical, spiritual or emotional hurts, pains and wounds. Compassion is usually seen as having an emotional dimension. But, in fact, it is more often expressed in systemic and structural modes, being rooted in concepts of fairness, justice, mutual interdependence and human flourishing. Humility and compassion is the act of St Martin of Tours cutting his cloak in two for the beggar in the gate. It is an act of mercy; a work of charity; an instinct, but also calculated. It is rooted in the heart, of course; but also rational in nature; an application understood as an activity based on sound judgement. Jesus' humility, passion, and his com-passion, are both calculated and matters of the heart. They are invariably risky prophetic acts that offend norms and sensibilities (the apparently moral and religious ones of his day), in order to reach out to people, and show others just how *much* God loves the poor, lame, outcast, demonized, sinner and marginalized.

So, compassion actually has a *quantitative* dimension. The compassion of an individual can have a property or character to it, such as depth, vigour, determination or altruism. The etymology of the term 'compassion' comes from the Latin word, meaning 'co-suffering'. To have com-passion is to suffer alongside, and so very deeply with, the very ones we seek to help. We enter into their experience. Just as Christ, in his com-passion, fully entered into our flesh; he became like us. And ultimately experienced the same scorn and hatred in his flesh that had been inflicted upon so many of the victims he had healed, loved and nurtured. Christ's incarnation and our redemption are rooted in God's passion for us; and his com-passion poured into the one who loved us enough to fully abide with us: Christ, no less.

Compassion, then, is much, much more involved than any mere empathy. And the one who has compassion, commonly, has an active desire to alleviate the suffering of another, to save and free them – sometimes from sin, but quite often from those alienating, visceral forces of hatred that oppress and marginalize people – and to which Jesus was (and is) so openly opposed. Yet too often, through pride and hubris, the church and its leaders fail in the deep calling to become 'wounded healers'. Too often, further damage is inflicted by a church represented by unhealed wounders.

As Harvey Cox noted in *On Not Leaving it to the Snake*, the first and original sin is not disobedience. It is, rather, indifference. We can no longer ignore the abuse – and the subsequent pain and alienation that others in the church experience – and especially when this is *because* of the church. Indifference is pitiful, and it is the enemy of compassion. Our age may well be one of anger, austerity and anxiety, but it is in such times that the church needs to recover its primary calling and roots. Rooted, indeed, in the one who was compassionate with us, and in Christ, continues to call us to full, loving humanity, one with another.

Disaster Control, Risk Management and Hazard Aversion

Back in 2017, the UK fell silent for two minutes at 11 a.m. for an act of remembrance that was nothing to do with great wars and losses of the twentieth century. We were instead remembering the victims of the fire in Grenfell Tower, London, with a loss of life exceeding 80 people. Even before the commencement of the public inquiry, it was clear that the disaster was partially caused by our old friend, 'deregulation'. It was David Cameron, as British Prime Minister, who pledged to 'kill off the safety culture for good' with another 'bonfire of red tape'. Since 2010, a third of UK environmental health officers have been lost, resulting in less checks of food outlets, less protection of landfill sites, and the closing of air quality stations. Our health and safety inspectorate has endured a near 50 per cent cut, in most workplaces.

But here's the thing. Good government and governance are made of red tape. It is the thread in the very fabric of civilization. But quite literally, it is the ribbon that binds the legal documents drawn up by your democratically elected representatives. Red tape is what binds us together as a society.

Red tape stops some abusing others; it stops employers maltreating employees or polluting the environment; it prevents rogue business undercutting good business; it keeps us safe; protects children and vulnerable adults; guarantees the food we eat; safeguards the medicines we take and the professional standards of lawyers, doctors or engineers that we rely on for life itself. Yes, it was the inadequacy of the red tape that killed the Grenfell victims. As one journalist put it:

> in all aspects of the working of the state, it takes eternal vigilance to stop officious or inept regulation: human devices are prone to human fallibility. But red tape is the history of progress, from factory acts keeping children out of mills, mines, and chimneys, to the limiting of working hours, and the granting of holidays, sick pay, and parental leave. (Toynbee, 2017, p. 15)

Much must change in the aftermath of the Grenfell disaster – the UK's towering inferno. May the ongoing review and judgement of all churches in every nation be a willing participant in that change-culture that leads to better practice, and to much better governance, transparency and oversight. For we recall not only acts of abuse and tragedy, but also the unexpected actions that we can't fully explain. Forgetfulness is actually the enemy of justice, and the destroyer of societies.

The task that now beckons is not 'forgive and forget', but 'remember and forgive'. It is important that we never forget; but equally important that we move and strive to forgive. It is only by accepting the past, claimed T. S. Eliot, that we can alter its meaning and power. In the UK, we have witnessed a series of disturbing revelations relating to the sexual abuse of minors and vulnerable adults, at the hands of media celebrities, prominent figures in public life, and the churches. Sir Jimmy Savile OBE is just one egregious reminder of how cultures of sexual abuse can hide in plain sight for decades. It was a 'mokita' phenomenon, as anthropologists might term it: 'what everyone knows, but no one says'. But there can be no excuse for power silencing truth, and the asphyxiation of valid testimonies. Too often, churches are willing to defer to the power and authority of bishops, often because they are perceived to hold 'ace cards': mystique, preferment and wider bases of knowledge. Yet we have tended to trust their assertions far more than is wise. We assume bishops to be almost omniscient. Yet, there must be significant doubts about their competencies in areas that they have had little if any professional training in – the safeguarding of children is an obvious arena.

Bishops often retain positions of 'oversight' in fields they simply do not comprehend: education, safeguarding, public policy – to name but a few. They feel the need to defend their comprehensiveness and role in such oversight, even when it is manifestly the case that they are out of their depth, or sometimes just wrong. All too often, exposure of any weakness, failure or wrongdoing is met with defensive assertions and reassertions. Then the awkwardness of the truth surfacing can become seemingly impossible, for no one knows what to say about what everyone actually knows. The elephant is now living in the room, but we talk past it every day. As Emma Percy's poem notes,

> We never planned to have an elephant.
> Our house is not designed for so large a pet.
> At best it would be chaotic,
> At worst, destructive.
> Don't get me wrong,
> Elephants are magnificent beasts in the right place:
> The plains of Africa
> The jungles of Sri Lanka
> Yet here we are with an Elephant in the room,
> Now occupying our living space.
>
> At first we assumed that we could easily rehome the elephant,
> Unravel the misunderstanding that led to its arrival.
>
> Yet it seems rehoming and re-ravelling are more complicated.
>
> The elephant inevitably took up space
> It trampled on the plants
> And defecated in the borders.
> It wanted to be near us
> But once inside the room
> Its bulk made conversation difficult,
> Obscuring the view and blocking the light.
>
> Though people tried to politely ignore it
> Our lives became shaped by its presence.
>
> People began to forget that we had not
> Asked for an Elephant.
> Despite having the paperwork showing
> Its origins, and our lack of ownership,
> It was assumed to be our elephant.
> After all, it lived in our house.

And so this is how we live,
Negotiating its size,
Tending to its needs,
And hoping daily for news of an Elephant sanctuary.
(Percy, 'The Elephant in the Room', 2020)

When it comes to dealing with elephants living in our houses and institutions, we should remember that truth must come before reconciliation. I am reminded of Desmond Tutu commenting in 1986: 'If you are neutral in situations of injustice, you have chosen the side of the oppressor. If an elephant has its foot on the tail of a mouse and you say that you are neutral, the mouse will not appreciate your neutrality.' When our courage is replaced with complicity, and compassion with empathy, you can perhaps understand my sense of betrayal and disgust.

In their intriguing book *Mistakes Were Made – But Not By Me*, Carol Tavris and Elliot Aronson explain how it is that the individuals and institutions that make catastrophic errors that cause damage and pain to others, or simply mistreat them, can live with themselves and justify their actions or inaction. The key to this they argue, is the individuals or institutions responsible for the neglect or abuse are able to calm their cognitive dissonance by creating fictions that absolve themselves of responsibility. Thus, the belief that we are clever, moral and right simply masks behaviours that are idiotic, immoral and wrong (Tavris and Aronson, 2008).

Like many loyal servants of the Church of England, I have watched revelations of child sexual abuse tumble out over the past few years, and with a growing, troubling, deep sense of shame. This is a hard thing to admit to, and a hard thing to say. To know that you belong to a body where you can no longer believe or trust the account of the polity and practice that is being offered in defence of its behaviours by its own leaders. To know that the real victims in this tragic farce who are still waiting for basic, fundamental rights that should be givens for the church – recognition, remorse, repentance – are abused twice over. In the first instance, it is by their actual abuser. The second time, and far worse, is the subsequent abuse perpetrated by the church. For this is a church that can be deaf, dumb and blind – and seemingly wilfully indifferent to the suffering undergone by those abused – and then addresses this with little more than a veneer of safeguarding practice, which only further compounds the original act of abuse.

But there is something else troubling about the Bishop Peter Ball case too. The problems in safeguarding do not just stem from some poor professionalism and meagre managerialism. They are rooted in warped attitudes to gender and sexuality; cultures of obeisance that do not challenge or question the competence of clergy and bishops, and instead puts them on a pedestal; failures to invest in training for seminarians and clergy in the basics of law, good practices, and relevant social and psychological theory; patronizing attitudes towards laity; and lazy, naive assumptions about human nature. These things will not be fixed by hiring a few more safeguarding officers. The problem runs far deeper and extends far wider.

The Church of England has not even begun to reckon with the ecclesial ethos and traditions that offered the best petri-dishes for developing and growing cultures of abuse. For decades, it has been easy for the church to point the finger of blame at liberals for lax standards and moral lapses. But the cultures of sexual abuse grew most successfully in traditionalist strains of Anglo-Catholicism (Bishop Peter Ball, for example) and biblicist strains of Conservative Evangelicalism (Jonathan Fletcher or John Smyth of their Iwerne Camps).

There are common denominators in these two deeply con-servative and traditionalist ecclesial cultures. They deny women equality. They are squeamish about sexuality, usually avoiding explicit discussion of the topic – except perhaps to condemn it – at any cost. They will sacralize certainty on some issues; and apotheosize ambiguity on other fronts. They put their leaders on unimpeachable pedestals and sacralize their priestly or preaching authority. They conflate the minister with the source of the minister's authority – namely Christ. To dispute with or question the integrity of the minister is to argue with God, and tantamount to heresy. The very worst kinds of abuses flourish in the cultures that are self-righteous.

In reflecting and writing, I have become aware that the abuses that victims suffer at the hands of the church will go unheeded, unless the church hands over its power and authority in safeguarding to a genuinely free and independent regulatory body. This is the only way that victims will be able to get the justice they deserve. It is the only way the churches can begin to rebuild public trust. Ultimately, we should look to a change of culture: one that many of us now believe is an urgent priority for churches. Without it, I fear for both victims and institution alike.

Conclusion

This whole agenda is work-in-progress. And to a large extent, any pastoral–theological perspective is bound, by definition, to be insufficient in relation to the issues we are facing here. These final remarks should be seen as preliminary, and as one small staging post along this lengthy viaticum.

First, let us remember where risk and responsibility come from. The word 'responsibility' comes from the Latin term, *respondere* meaning 'to be answerable' and 'to respond'. The word evolved to mean being 'accountable for one's actions' and 'reliable, trustworthy'; moreover, the word 'obligation' is in the Latin root word. 'Risk', in contrast, means 'to run into'. We might say there is no such thing as 'responsible risk' with our most vulnerable. To be responsible means to be risk aversive, to avoid taking chances.

Second, repentance means turning away from practices, habits and sins. Not 360 degrees, because that would bring us back on ourselves. Repentance is a full turning away; a setting aside of all that inhibits. It is making a conscious and determined decision – of body, mind, heart and spirit – to not repeat the past. Repentance is what the churches are called to here, in relation to abuse. Apologies are not enough. Neither is contrition. Repentance is the way forward. Sorrow for the past; determination for the future.

Third, the body of Christ was richly incarnate. Christ, in his healing ministry, usually heard the unheard, saw the unseen, could speak for the silent, could feel the unfelt. This body of Christ had a keen sense for the abused and the marginalized, and often placed such people at the heart of his ministry, to interrogate and speak to crowds and witnesses on their role in colluding with the stigmatization of the needy. The healing was not just physical, but social and judicial. We are called to this same work of healing and deliverance.

Poet Heather Pencavel's poem 'Roadbuilding', is based on the call to 'prepare the way', uttered by John the Baptist in Luke 3.4:

> Roadbuilding is rough work
> hard labour, muscles strained
> hands calloused, back near breaking
> even with lifting gear, hard hat, protective boots.
> Site clearance is dirty work and dangerous
> removing rotten structures,
> risking unsafe ground
> uncovering long-forgotten corruption,
> the stink too strong to breathe
> of waste and dereliction.
>
> God you cry out to us
> to clear the site, build the road
> because you are coming
> and you will come
> along the road we build.
> Give your people, we pray
> the will and stamina for the job.
>
> Give us courage, to tackle the clearance
> of debt and exploitation
> which corrupt communities and nations.
> Give us the grit and determination
> to straighten out the crooked structures
> which make it hard for the poor and the weak
> to journey to freedom –

And help us to shout aloud that you will come
along the road we build.
(Pencavel, 'Roadbuilding', 2019)

We now need to change the culture of the church – so history
does not repeat itself with prevailing patterns of abuse, defensive assertions and cover-ups. The Church of England – in fact
all churches, where this is possible – need to actively hand over
child protection and safeguarding matters to a single independent authority. So, not an authority churches control, but one
rather they would be subject to. This is quite normal for public
life – with press, advertising, and energy companies, among
others – are all regulated by bodies in the interests of ensuring
fair and transparent public service and basic ethical standards.

There is a close, embedded – some may say incestuous –
relationship between the insurers of the churches, and church
leaders who have a role in governing and overseeing the insurance companies. So, bishops and others are often compromised
on areas of liability, apology and pay-outs to victims. They
cannot be pastors to victims and directors or financial beneficiaries of the insurance companies that may pay-out on claims.
These spheres and functions need separating. We need an Independent Regulator now for all the churches, so we no longer
do it for ourselves. It is clear we can't manage the burden of
this any more – morally or responsibly. Church is a sacred
space, but also public space; it is not a private sect.

So, may almighty God give us grace and wisdom to make the
rough places smooth, the barren places spring to life, and the
crooked paths straight. In so doing, may we redeem the time,
the church, and those whom we've lost and put in harm's way.
May almighty God give us grace to listen, repent, and resolve
to work for a Kingdom of Righteousness that serves those we
have wronged.

Smoking in Public

> One thing is clear to me: the temptation of power is greater
> when intimacy is a threat. Much Christian leadership is exer-
> cised by people who do not know how to develop healthy,
> intimate relationships and have opted for power and control
> instead.
> *Henri Nouwen*

As an undergraduate, I was taught moral philosophy by a
Roman Catholic Marxist, who was passionate about liberation
theology, had a deep admiration for the proto-communism of
the seventeenth-century Levellers and Diggers, as well as the
later nineteenth-century Chartists. His lectures were poignant,
wise, funny, rich, provocative and unforgettable. He lectured,
as many did in those days, chain-smoking his way through
explaining the finer points of Platonic and Aristotelian ethics
and introducing us to obscure German philosophers. Dressed
from head-to-toe in black – skinny jeans, baggy old black
sweater (with patches, naturally), black denim jacket and
receding jet-black hair – his manner sometimes resembled a
kind of Max Wall offering regular recitals of The Communist
Manifesto.

Once, apropos nothing, he turned to the class and asked if
anyone minded him smoking? As it turned out, no one did;
or if they did, no one said. But he went on to say that if one
person objected, just one, then he would not do so. He went
on to explain that his smoking in class was not a democratic
decision: that a 51 to 49 per cent vote in favour of continuing
to smoke would make it right for us all. Basic human rights,
he explained, were above democratic decisions, and there were
many things that should not be determined by the popular will

of the people: capital punishment for example, or discrimination on grounds of gender, ethnicity, disability and sexuality were also mentioned. To make the point, he stubbed out his cigarette, and said that we could not do ethics if we did not start from the basis that everyone was equal, and that meant some things you might want to do – your desires or apparent choices – were not necessarily exercises in democracy, but if pursued could be construed as anti-society.

Behind this rather stark observation lay a serious point: what does mutual flourishing mean? It must mean, surely, he argued, that some of my freedoms, desires and choices have to be sacrificed for the common good. Smoking was a small example, he added. Slavery or apartheid served as better illustrations. Voting for both could never make either right.

Gender, Equality and Mutuality

The *Report of the Review of Nomination to the See of Sheffield* by Sir Philip Mawer was published in September 2017. The Report set out the findings of a review requested by the Archbishops of Canterbury and York following the announcement that the Bishop of Burnley, Philip North, had withdrawn from nomination to the Diocese of Sheffield. This 75-page Report drew from meetings with and personal submissions from more than 100 people (including over 60 from the Sheffield Diocese) over recent months seeking to learn lessons from the events surrounding Bishop North's nomination to and subsequent withdrawal from the See.

The debate over the debacle in the See of Sheffield, and the subsequent Report, represented a clash of languages and cultures. It was not a binary clash, either. There were several conflictual cultures at work buffering up against one another. Conservative Catholics; accommodating liberals who want to make concessions to conservatives; campaigning liberals who don't want to make concessions; gender binaries and dialects; progressives and traditionalists; theologians and those representing party interests; and then an institutional culture that can't resolve the disputes, so resorts to the language of arbitration, but refuses to make any kind of discerning judgements on the theological merits of cases involved in the disputes.

This leads to the present problem, namely the Church of England's inability to distinguish between quality and efficacy in competing theological convictions and beliefs, which leads to some unfortunate ecclesial compromises. Thus, despite having a General Synod that votes on issues – not just on the basis of personal preferences, but also on the basis of the quality of theological arguments that convict and persuade – the actual decisiveness of such processes are robbed of their power by supplementary concessions.

This is unusual, slightly specious, and somewhat un-Catholic behaviour on the part of the Church of England. All the great Councils and Synods of the church, for the best part of 2,000 years, have deliberated, debated and then voted on matters that threatened to divide the church. There were no post-vote accommodations for the Gnostics in the second century; or for the Arians in the fourth century. These groups had argued their cases on the nature of Christ – and they lost those arguments. A decision was made. The church chose the path of the orthodox, better-quality, more persuasive theological arguments. That is what Synods and Councils do.

The Church of England did exactly the same with women priests in 1992, and women bishops in 2013. One cannot pretend the result was really a 'score draw'. It wasn't. Yet accommodations and provisions were nonetheless made in 1993, to those who could not in conscience accept women priests. Reparations for those defeated is honourable and good, conveying important and authentic signals about future hopes of togetherness. But it ends there. One cannot, as I think Philip Mawer's arbitration unconsciously scripts, pretend that these competing convictions were and are of equal theological value and weight. If they were, the voting would tell us that, and there would be stalemate, and no women priests or bishops in the Church of England. The fact that women priests and bishops now exist proves beyond a shadow of doubt that the Church of England worked through this theological and ecclesial disputation – and with principles and methods utterly consistent with the great Councils and Synods of the wider Catholic Church.

Mawer's Report also revealed how far the centre of gravity in the Church of England had drifted from the general public and contemporary culture. We are informed that 'prominent voices question(ed) the nomination including those of Lord Blunkett and the MP for Sheffield Heeley, Ms Louise Haigh' (para. 66). This is a highly significant issue for public theology and an established Church – not least for its public witness and Christian credibility. The sentence above, however, is the only mention of this exceptional, probably unparalleled intervention by a former Labour Government Minister and Peer, and a serving Member of Parliament. The intervention merited some serious discussion, and not merely a fleeting mention. The Report revealed a church talking to itself, relatively deaf to wider culture.

The centre of gravity for the Report lies in several interlocking loci. First, how the church seeks to manage an unresolvable ecclesial conflict, and competing theological convictions. The Report is at pains to stress how the way ahead can (somehow) be managed. The document cannot, of course, go into the deep theological divisions that underpin the issues. But it should be obvious by now – 25 years after the vote to ordain women to the priesthood at the November 1992 General Synod – that the weight of theological arguments for and against the ordination of women are not of equal *value*, and so cannot easily be 'balanced' in any ecclesial context. And even if the Bishops and General Synod likes to think that these arguments are of equal weight, the rest of the Church of England, general public and wider culture think differently on this debate. The issue is plain. How does the Church of England honour, protect and affirm a (small) *dissenting minority*? A minority, moreover, that should not be able to impose their dissenting views on a non-consenting majority?

Second, that 'normative' voice in the Report, and in the church it speaks for and of, is essentially an adult male supporting the ordination of women, but also trying to affirm, appease or compensate those who are, in conscience against women's ordination. Hence, paragraph 115 states that 'the difficulty about this latter suggestion' (that is, the proposal to reserve a place for an ordained woman on the CNC) argues that 'if there is to be a reserved place for a woman, why not set aside reserved places for *others* too?' Women, despite being half the population, and a majority of our churchgoers, are being presented as part of this group known as 'others' – supplementary interest groups and minorities.

Third, the issue of discrimination on grounds of gender in the Report still receives little attention. Indeed, the term 'discrimination' is not used in the Report once, except when quoting my own writing. 'Sexism' and 'sexist' get a single mention each – again, only quoting those who are protesting against gender-based discrimination. The Report fails to acknowledge that gender – just like age, sexuality or ethnicity – is regarded by the law and wider society as 'protected characteristics'. That is to say, people can do little about who they are. But faith-based convictions are hardly in the same category. True, religious beliefs do enjoy some measure of protection under the law. But that protection does not extend to allowing those beliefs to be imposed on others – and especially without their full and clear consent.

That is why, of course, congregations, the wider public, and many clergy, were right to question and challenge the nomination of any person to the See of Sheffield, who could not affirm his women clergy, and their full sacramental validity and efficacy. The law, and indeed the church, will defend his right to his conscience and his views. But there is no case for entitling or privileging those who hold such convictions. And most especially, to place persons with such views in a position of oversight above others – who in turn would be adversely affected and impacted by such discriminatory views. (Assurances of 'affirmation' for those who might be impacted are simply inadequate, and entirely miss the point. The remedy against discrimination cannot be compensatory gestures and pastoral assurances, if inequality is allowed to remain in place.)

Fourth, the Report accepts, uncritically, that proponents of 'traditionalist' views clearly doubt the sacramental efficacy of women priests and bishops, and in no uncertain terms (para. 72). But the rationale for this is puzzling:

> The basis of ... objection to women's ordination is the authority and unity of the Church. The Church of England is part of the one holy catholic Church of God and that imposes limits on what it can and can't decide unilaterally. Extending the historic threefold order to women constitutes a major doctrinal change and thus, while it may be the way the Spirit is calling the Church, it is an action that the Church of England does not have the unilateral authority to undertake. (para. 141)

It is odd to single out ordination as the factor in the 'authority and unity' of the One Holy Catholic Church (Roman Catholic and Orthodox). The official teaching of the Roman Catholic Church on the sanctity of life – conception, contraception and so forth – and the proper ordering of family life are major tenets of Catholicism. The Church of England departed from such positions decades ago – 'decide(ing) unilaterally' – that managing the size of a family through artificial means (contraception) was not wrong or sinful. Roman Catholic orthodoxy disagrees. So why do traditionalist Anglicans choose to ignore one major Roman Catholic doctrine, but not others? Indeed, there are many other 'essential' Roman Catholic doctrines and teachings that Anglicans have not assented to for many centuries. So, it is somewhat specious to draw one line in the sand with women priests and women bishops.

Religion and Public Life – Exceptionalism and Egalitarianism

So, what of the relationship between smoking and faith? Churches have never had a comfortable relationship with this social habit. Alcohol in churches and on church premises – not for all denominations, granted – barely raises an eyebrow.

But no denomination, to the best of my knowledge, has ever installed ashtrays in the pews. As the apocryphal story has it, a young Roman Catholic priest asks his bishop if he may smoke while he prays. The bishop says, firmly, 'no'. A Jesuit brother asks the same bishop 'can I pray while I smoke?' to which the answer is 'absolutely, yes'. This is a can-you-have-your-cake-and-eat-it conundrum. And in a world of busy religious consumerism, it pitches exceptionalism against egalitarianism. Exceptionalism will expect to be treated differently, and perhaps even better than others – but at any rate, have their rights privileged and protected. An egalitarian will favour equality: people should get the same, or be treated the same, or be treated as equals. Egalitarianism builds from the concept of social equality for all people. Egalitarian 'doctrines' are formed from the foundation that all humans are equal in fundamental worth and moral status.

The Church of England, broad and tolerant as it is, can be confused by this. Indeed, this is inchoately reflected in the Mawer Report – a tangled and muddled spaghetti of concerns that lack the clear ethical principles that should underpin its work, and hold together the intrinsic worth of people who hold to dissenting minority opinions, and the majority of public who hold to the moral consensus that binds society. Three brief examples will suffice here, to illustrate this point.

First, most orthodox Sikhs wear the *dastaa*r – the turban-like headgear being an article of faith that connotes identity, spirituality and piety. As a religious-ethnic article, it qualifies for exemptions under the law. Many countries in the developed world allow Sikhs not to wear crash helmets on motorbikes. But the law does not permit a Sikh motorbike instructor to insist that any who take lessons from him discard their helmet and wear a *dastaa*r instead. Sikhs have liberty of conscience – but not the right to impose this on others. There are limits to the liberty of conscience too. Many developed countries do not permit the wearing of *dastaa*r on building sites in place of hard hats. The argument being that more than one person's safety and well-being is compromised, potentially, by an individual wanting to exercise their liberty of conscience. The law

challenges that. In the same way, a minister holding comple-
mentarian views on the place of women in church, marriage
and ministry, cannot order their local church school on the
same basis. Parents, pupils and staff would not consent to the
imposition of such a theonomy.

Second, we turn to food. It would be reasonable to go to
a family restaurant and only order and eat vegetarian food.
But it would be unreasonable to complain about the other
diners who were eating meat or fish. It is reasonable to request
a vegetarian option at a steakhouse; and no good steakhouse
would be without such choices on the menu. It would be
unreasonable and rude to go to a vegetarian restaurant and
request a rare-cooked steak. It would be reasonable to take
over a restaurant and manage it as it was, attracting the same
custom, especially if it was the only one of its kind for miles
around. But less reasonable for the new manager (please note,
not the owner) to refuse to offer simple food that was once
on the menu, because it troubled the manager's conscience.
It would not be reasonable to differentiate between diners,
dividing the vegetarians from the meat eaters at tables. Or to
exalt those on special diets at the expense of the majority of
other customers.

In both of these examples, there is something here to note
about permissiveness and the liberty of conscience in a broad
society. The needs and requirements of a minority, as we can
see, are honoured and provided for. No one orders a steak
in a vegetarian restaurant in the same way that no one ever
seriously asks 'where is the female celebrant?' at a Forward
in Faith church or a congregation run by The Society. Here,
in such places and spaces, minority views are protected and
can be affirmed. But the will of this minority cannot be easily
exported to or shared with others, where it will offend, let
alone become *determinative* for the majority.

This brings us to smoking – our third example – and my
tutor in moral philosophy, who has now given up smoking
entirely. But as he notes, a minority of people still like to
smoke cigarettes. Smoking remains lawful. But restrictions on
smoking in enclosed public spaces is legislature that came into

force in 2007. Society reached a mind – by majority – on how the personal choices of a very few – a minority – might infringe the liberty of *all*. Smoking in public spaces was no longer a 'private matter' – an issue for the conscience or manners of the smoker, to make a judgement on how nearby non-smokers or children might react. Smoking in public is deemed to be 'anti-social', and the legislation recognizes that one person's liberty to smoke infringes on the well-being of others.

Discriminatory views on grounds of race, gender and disability are similar. You may think what you like in private: but you can't implement such views and practices on the public. So, smokers remain free to light-up in private. But they are no longer free to share (or inflict) their habit on the wider public. Smokers effectively lost their familiar freedoms – so that wider society could gain equality of experience with fresh air in enclosed shared spaces. There was no feasible compromize.

It was not illiberal to regard 'designated smoking zones' inside restaurants as offensive and antisocial. Nor would it be 'illiberal liberalism' to resist new requests for alternative shared spaces being opened up for smokers, in order to compensate for their loss of old customary public places. We don't seek to balance the losses of privilege for smokers by yielding them some new public space. We don't say, 'Well, we banned smoking in all pubs, but as reparation, you can now smoke in certain restaurants.' Or, for that matter, set about redesignating all trains as smoking zones once again, and reintroduce specified non-smoking carriages. Nor do we suggest that smokers can light up in *your* private space, which was hitherto smoke-free.

As for passive smoking and public spaces, the claim that smokers only impact their own health has been widely refuted. In the same vein, a male bishop opposed to women priests will invariably have a widespread impact on the 'air' of the whole diocese – clergy and laity alike – quite independent of any personal or public compensatory gestures they attempt to make. That's because theological positions are inherently influential and powerful. They are liminal and subliminal; explicit and implicit. Theology affects mood and morale. Even privately held theological convictions will send unconscious coded signals that shape culture, churches and congregations: communicating acceptance or rejection, faith, or doubt. So, we need to know that our bishops fully affirm the ministry of *all* their clergy – irrespective of their gender.

That said, there have been compensatory measures. The provision of Parochial Episcopal Visitors (also known as 'flying bishops') allows for dissenting congregations to be adequately cared for. This is prudent provision for a minority view, and has much to commend it. But as for the rest of the Church of England, please note that the guidance from the secular world is that cultures only begin to shift in organizations, corporations and institutions when the leaders, board of executives or directors exceeds around 35 per cent in terms of female representation (McKinsey & Company, 2012). Women bishops currently number less than 10 per cent of our total number. In fact, the number of women bishops is about the same as the number of bishops who oppose women priests and women bishops.

In terms of power and parity today, the faith-based opinions of a few in the church, and amounting to opposition to unequivocal equality, does not mean that the opponents of gender-based equality should now somehow still expect to be met halfway in this debate. Gender equality is either equality, or it is nothing. Furthermore, it is not 'illiberal' to oppose gender-based discrimination. To be liberal does not commit you to accepting every shade of opinion as equally valid.

Moreover, a commitment to equality often demands the sacrifice and self-denial of a minority, for the wider common good of all. Sometimes, such sacrifice is *not* reciprocal. Indeed, establishing of equality can require one group to sacrifice a great deal – possibly even *all* their power and privileges. At the same time, the beneficiaries of this may sacrifice little or nothing in return for their newly found equality.

So, it could never be 'illiberal-liberalism' to oppose the appointment of a pro-apartheid politician as the new government minister for education. It would simply be rational to object to such an appointment, quite independent of their other qualities and gifts. The apartheid regime divided educational opportunity according to the colour of people's skin. The new South Africa does not, and assumes all should be educated equally, independent of ethnicity. There is no halfway house.

If the Church of England can't commit to the equality of women, then it will always be difficult to attribute conviction and weight to other equality-based interventions on social policy and wider welfare matters. The culture of the church needs to embrace equality unequivocally. We have to be clear that although our church is sacred space, it is also a very public place. Our church is the public's spiritual body; it needs to correspond to the best standards in public life.

The church is a 'community of contrast'; it is not of the world. So, it is called to operate with and incorporate far higher standards and values than those the world would normally settle for. The main question against the Mawer Report is ultimately this: does it put the church *before* the Kingdom of God?

The Church of England's ecclesial modus operandi – short-term treaties that compromise others – seems to be some way off the 'ecclesial community of equality' imagined by the Apostle Paul: 'there is no longer Jew or Greek, there is no longer slave or free, there is no longer male and female; for all of you are one in Christ Jesus' (Galatians 3.28). Jesus did not institute the church; he *constituted* a kingdom community. In using the word 'constitute' here, I mean he embodied and lived 'kingdom values', showing partiality not just towards the poor and marginalized, but also and especially to women of all kinds (Jew, Gentile, etc.). If we are, as the archbishop says (quoted in para. 95 of the Report) 'to (remember) at all times that our identity is in Christ alone', then we will remember too that our common humanity is rooted in the equality Christ taught, and the early church caught, by raising up women who led churches, mission and ministry – Phoebe, Tabitha, Junia and Priscilla – and more besides.

Emma Percy's poem, 'The Body of Christ', captures the mutuality inherent in the actuality of the life and practice of the incarnation:

Jesus' body was a male body,
A Palestinian Jew, circumcised on the eighth day,
muscled from manual labour, weathered by an itinerant
   ministry.
The body of Christ is black hands,
calloused from work in the fields, clapping a rhythm of praise.
The body of Christ is the tired feet
of the nurse at the end of the day entrusting the sick to the
   mercy of God.
The body of Christ is the foreshortened arm
offering hospitality, reaching far beyond the physical
   limitations.
The body of Christ is the breast full of milk which suckles
   the child,
the womb which bleeds and contains new life.
The body of Christ is eyes, blue, green, brown
looking with compassion on the poor of the world,
ears that hear the voices of the voiceless.
The body of Christ is the mind
capable of exploring the heights and depths of theology,
the voice that speaks blessings in many languages,
the laughter of companions,
the sighs of lovers, the silence of contemplation.
The body of Christ is male and female and intersex.
The body of Christ is straight and gay, single and married,
   old and young, rich and poor, lost and found.
The body of Christ is risen and redeemed;
a multiplicity of human diversity working together for
   the kingdom.
We are the body of Christ,
for in one spirit we were all baptized
into one body.
(Percy, 'The Body of Christ', 2017)

Conclusion

A laudable goal for gender equality and justice in the Church of England would ideally aim for one third of our bishops being women before any more 'traditionalists' are appointed to Diocesan Sees. Indeed, we should try and work towards half our bishops being women by 2037 – 50 years after women were first ordained as deacons. We still have many, many miles to travel on such a journey. Our current equivocal attitude to women in the church can only slow that journey down even more, and it might even send us backwards. Instead, we really do need to move forward – in faith.

A letter from the Revd Dr Joanna Collicutt (Karl Jaspers Lecturer in Psychology of Religion and Spirituality, Cuddesdon) to the *Church Times* in October 2017 is salutary on precisely these points:

> Sir, An approximate frequency count of words referring to key people in the Mawer Report (News, 22 September; Letters, 29 September) yields interesting findings. Bishop Philip North is mentioned 211 times. Professor Martyn Percy is mentioned 83 times. The word 'women' occurs 144 times, but only 43 of these occurrences refer to actual women.
>
> The majority use of the word 'women' is conceptual, as in 'women's ordination', 'women's ministry', or 'women bishops'. In these instances, the concept is frequently referred to as an 'issue', a 'matter', or a 'subject' on which people might take a view or position, either recognizing and receiving it, or not. Here the word 'women' forms part of an object that is to be considered and does not signify a voice that is to be heard.
>
> The Report is written by a man. There are 24 appendices. Of these, 13 are written by men, eight by committees, two are administrative, and one is written by a woman.
>
> As the Americans say, 'You do the math', or as St Matthew wrote, 'Let the reader understand.'

The Church of England's 'Five Guiding Principles' turn out to be engaging in what the French playwright Alfred Jarry called 'the science of imaginary solutions'. The Five Principles, and indeed Philip Mawer's Report, do not recognize the inherent gender-blindness they contain, and that remains present within the polity of the Church of England. More broadly, the Church of England seems not to have learned from church history. If the laudable desire for catholicity and unity are placed above doctrine – or the intrinsic value, worth and equality of humanity – then the truth cannot be served. It is a lesson the early church constantly learned over creeds and councils. It was a lesson – a long one – learned by the American Episcopal Church on slavery during the American Civil War (1861–65). Desiring not to descend into schism, and desiring to preserve catholicity at all costs, Episcopalians prized unity in the midst of sharp political difference above affirming the inherent equality and value of all humans. So, despite slavery being a cause of the American Civil War, its contributory racism went largely unchallenged by Episcopalians, for fear of offending Confederate Christians. When the war ended, little was said about slavery or racism by the church. The one bishop consecrated by the breakaway Confederates was allowed to join the ranks of the reunited Episcopalian bishops. Nothing more was said: unity preserved, but the divisive racism that had caused the war was conveniently ignored.

There are some who believe that the 'mutual flourishing' the Church of England seeks is a permissive licence to promote a kind of 'internalized ecumenism'. As for mutual flourishing, I believe it can work, provided we remember that the term 'mutual' means that things that are held in common are common, and there is reciprocity between the holders. Yet the word 'mutual' cannot imply that all views are *equally* valid and valuable. Once the Church of England has grasped that, we might all begin to move on. And I daresay, flourish.

PART THREE

Christ and Christianity

'Us and Them':
One Body, One Bread

Never look down on anybody unless you're helping them up.
Jesse Jackson

The fallout from the English Civil War of 1642–49 (or, the English Revolution) lasted for generations, and was devastating for the economy, society and humanity. This period also saw the emergence of a plethora of sects and movements that grew out of the social dis-ease. We forget far too easily, what a catastrophe that war wrought on Great Britain and Ireland. The war had spread, virally, from England to Scotland and Wales, and then to Ireland. More lives were lost in these 'civil' wars from 1642–52, as a percentage of the British population, than the two World Wars combined. A squabble about theocracy and democracy ended with the death of a monarch, Charles I. Yet the Commonwealth under Cromwell quickly morphed into a new, darker form of theocracy. One dictator replaced another.

Today, we cannot really comprehend the scale of this national trauma. It was shocking in the scale of violence. Not least because the war divided communities and families bitterly and irrevocably: fathers against sons; mothers against daughters; brothers and sisters divided; neighbours feuded; clergy and laity took different sides; villages and towns declared for one cause, and so against another. Amid this, many innocent civilians caught up in the conflict were slaughtered. Many were starved, imprisoned or exiled.

What would have been perplexing for many then, as now, was that there was no way of clearly identifying your enemy, except through the conflict. Protestants and Catholics look alike. There was no marked difference in appearance between Royalists and Parliamentarians. Families may have resemblances in appearances on the outside, but on the inside, there may be bitter ideological, theological and political rivalries. Our neighbours are nearly always 'othered;' and the chances are if we don't do it them, they'll most likely do it to us.

Them-and-Us may be one of the defining divisions of our age. We tend to regard ourselves as 'normative', and those unlike us as 'other'. Prejudicial labels abound. Think 'straight' and its (historic) opposites: 'bent' or 'queer'. Think in terms of black and white; British or American citizen, and the alleged opposites – 'immigrant', 'illegal', 'alien', 'migrant'. Think 'male' (normal) and 'female' (different). As humans, we can't help ourselves trying to process, order, categorize and evaluate what and who we see, and what may matter and what may not. To do so is merely to be a rational creature. However, we often forget that what we think is our *description* is very often our *ascription* too. What and whom we see are always *weighted* – socially, morally, emotionally – in ways we are seldom conscious of (our unconscious bias). This because the mind settles, if it can, on what is 'normative', and that alone allows us to determine what is 'other', unusual or atypical.

Yet the future Jesus proclaims in the coming of the Kingdom, and the equality embodied in the early church, transcended the conscious and unconscious – those mental walls of categorization and bias that exist within even the most generous hearts and reflective minds. The future Jesus advocated and advanced in ministry and mission – the new kingdom that was to come – gave us a foretaste of God's ultimate goal of harmony, peace and love. In the meantime, we are bid, as followers of God to usher in as the church, the *kin*-dom of God. *Kin*-dom is not a pun. The phrase 'kith and kin' is ancient. 'Kith' describes groups of people who just happen to live close, or in our network or community: it refers to those whom we choose to be friends with. 'Kin', in contrast, refers to our 'nearest and dearest' – family – and whom we cannot choose.

Here is the rub, however. God in Christ adopts us all as children of God. In turn, the church is asked to become an adoptive agency for Christ's all-embracing reconciling love. Churches often run on lines of 'kith' – we choose the congregation we want to be part of, and the fellowship we keep. But 'kin' is stronger. It is to become a community where we are asked to love those we dislike; bless and pray for our enemies; share bread with those with whom we might have sharp differences. The church is a call to kinship; to develop kindred relations; we are asked not to settle for mere kith in our congregations.

In this new world, we are all interrelated. The church is all about kin, not kith. There is to be no otherness in this new religious movement. Alterity is abolished in Jesus. This poem from Steve Lodewyke, who moved to Britain as a child, having been born in Sri Lanka, gets to the significant part:

I know otherness. It's who I am.
But it's not who I want to be
No Sir, it's not who I want to be.

Sir, what's with all this African American?
British Asian?
Indigenous Australian?
BAME?
It's otherness. Always otherness.

To you I am a compound, not the pure.
Not the shining, white light of elemental belonging,
To you, I am tarnished and base.
That's why I'm given that name.
That's why I am otherness.

My Dad told me to work hard
and keep my nose clean.
But no one cares.
It cuts no ice with my otherness.
My good deeds, my high IQ, my love for people,
None of it can be seen on my skin,
Only my otherness, writ bold and black.

So, Sir, you have won.
I capitulate.
I am done.
I am otherness.
And I will wriggle no more.
I will go quietly.
I won't knock at your door.
My place is otherness.
And I know my place.

Otherness.
It's as plain as the nose on my face.
(Lodewyke, 'Other', 2020)

In what follows, I explore the 'Them-and-Us' paradigm, and where Jesus stands in it. I have deliberately avoided applying this directly to Black Lives Matter, LGBTQ+ issues and identities, ethnic or national divisions, or able-dis-abled. Readers will be able to work out their own applications from the general and detailed reflections that are offered here, and I strongly encourage that. The questions – always – to ask when Jesus performs a miracle are: Who is this for? Why is this person in need of healing, and what has their affliction cost them? Where and when does the miracle take place – the actual place, times and within what location? How does the person who is healed fit into society, before, during and after the healing? What is the impact of the healing and restoration on the witnesses? What were the consequences then, and what are the consequences now?

Considering the Canaanite

In Mark (7.24–30) and in Matthew (15.21–31), Jesus is recorded as healing a Canaanite woman's daughter while travelling in the region of Phoenicia. Because of the faith shown by the woman, her request – her pleading – is signalled as a sign of extraordinary faith. Matthew's Gospel puts it like this:

Jesus left that place and went away to the district of Tyre and Sidon. Just then a Canaanite woman from that region came out and started shouting, 'Have mercy on me Lord, Son of David, my daughter is tormented by a demon.' But he did not answer her at all. And his disciples came and urged him, saying, '[Send her away],[9] for she keeps shouting after us.' He answered, 'I was sent only to the lost sheep of the house of Israel.' But she came and knelt before him, saying, 'Lord, help me.' He answered, 'It is not fair to take the children's food and throw it to the dogs.' She said, 'Yes, Lord; yet even the dogs eat the crumbs that fall from their masters' table.' Then Jesus answered her, 'Woman, great is your faith! Let it be done for you as you wish.' And her daughter was healed instantly. After Jesus had left that place, he passed along the Sea of Galilee, and he went up the mountain, where he sat down. Great crowds came to him bringing with them the lame, the maimed, the blind, the mute and many others. They put them at his feet, and he cured them.

For many readers of this text, there are three striking things to note. First, the apparent initial silence and indifference of Jesus. Second, the apparent insult of Jesus (he calls the woman a 'dog'). Third, the apparent haggling for healing that takes place, with the woman pleading for her daughter, while Jesus seems to imply, initially, that he is simply 'not here' for the likes of her, but only for 'the lost sheep of the house of Israel'. By chapter 15 of Matthew we are beginning to see signs of the tide turning against Jesus by the leaders of the country. Jesus is now turning more to the Gentiles. The situating of this healing story is pivotal. The chapter begins with a tetchy, even rude exchange between Jesus and his Jewish critics on questions of faith, food, purity and personhood, and ends with the feeding of 4,000 Gentiles. This chapter, therefore, is very much about sharing and entitlement. *Who* is this bread for?

Some scholars have suggested that the story of the Canaanite woman is a racist episode. That Jesus' silence is violence, and that this encounter with the woman is what changes Jesus and marks his moment of movement from exclusion to inclusion

(Alonso, 2011). For reasons that will become apparent, I do not share this view. I think the intentionality of Jesus' inclusiveness is rooted in the incarnation itself, and not a political or religious choice that Jesus makes in later life and ministry. That said, I am not entirely persuaded by the apparent dialectical inclusion-exclusion axis. For Christians, modelling the body of Christ, the better word is 'incorporation' – linked to the Latin concept of *corpus*, or *corporatus* – namely 'to form into a body'. Jesus, as God incarnate in Christ, is both incorporated and an incorporator.

For many years I have promoted a view that one of the primary concerns we should bear in mind when reading the accounts of Jesus' healing ministry in the Gospels (over 40 instances are listed), is not whether or not it ever happened. But rather, what were the social, political and religious pointers within such healings – for the person healed, and for the witnesses (Percy, 1996; Percy, 2017a, pp. 333–50). To put this more practically, and for future study, there are four questions to always ask:

1 Who is this miracle for (poor, tainted, lame, leper, etc.)?
2 What does the miracle involve (touch, conversation, etc.)?
3 Where and when does it happen (religious building [rare], Gentile or Jewish territory, on the Sabbath, after a long period of affliction, etc.)?
4 Why did Jesus heal this person, and in front of these witnesses, and for what ends (because they were marginalized, stigmatized, ostracized, etc.)?

When you read the healing miracles with these lenses, it quickly becomes apparent that Jesus rarely heals anyone with social pedigree or religious significance, his own friends or family, and in nearly every case, the person who is healed is so utterly insignificant that their names were never recorded in the Gospels.

The Canaanite woman fits the bill in every respect. Yet what I find peculiar about many Bible commentaries addressing this healing story is that they miss the obvious, dwelling on the wrong details. Some stress the persistence of the woman and the way it erodes Jesus' resolve, making him respond wearily. Some suggest that in so doing, Jesus is teaching her (and us) how to pray. Some commentators assert that Jesus ignores the woman. That is certainly what the disciples would have hoped for. But read the text more carefully, and we see that when the Canaanite woman calls out to Jesus, he at first says nothing. I do not think his 'silence is violence'; or that his apparent indifference is indicative. Matthew does not say that Jesus colludes with the request of the disciples for the woman to be silenced and sent away. Only that Jesus did not say a word in answer to her. Yet.

Jesus does hear; and yet at first, he refuses to answer. He is listening, but he delays his response. The apparent initial rejection by Jesus does not deter the woman in the least. Indeed, she offers Jesus homage as the 'Son of David' – as he is to her the Jewish king and Messiah. Worshipping Christ, she humbles herself before him – 'a humble and contrite heart, O God, thou wilt not despise'.

This explains her reference to 'crumbs under the table' – the same phrase we find in Cranmer's Prayer of Humble Access in the Book of Common Prayer. The woman says, 'Lord, yet even the dogs eat the crumbs that fall from their masters' table.' In so doing, she means to say, 'I am a worthless dog to your disciples and in the eyes of a Jewish rabbi like you. I am not worthy of the children's bread, who as a Gentile cannot be a guest at your table. Yet the dogs and the curs[10] eat the crumbs of bread which fall from the tables.' So, she is saying: 'Nourish me as your dog. I will not leave your table. You cannot drive me away.' (The illustration on pp. iii and 177 by Alice Woudhuysen, picturing a simple feast, with some pets, is now explained.)

Indeed, this is how to interpret the silence and hesitation of Jesus. He pauses. He is listening with both ears to two different kinds of noise: 'Get rid of her ... we can't stand the racket' and 'Please God, help me!' WWJD: What Would Jesus Do here? Exactly what you'd expect. He waits. Will the disciples complaining about the noise listen to the one pleading loudly? He lets her plead; but the disciples want her shut up and shut out. Jesus, in the end, engages – as no one else does –

and commends her faith, foreign-born and mongrel though it is. It shuts the disciples up. Jesus does the same with Samaritan woman at the well and the demoniac of Gerasene. Jesus goes out of his way to engage the faith of those outside Judaism. He is an itinerant boundary-crosser

That said, Jesus' comparison to the woman as a 'dog' is hardly friendly. There is no way of reading Jesus' remarks other than as derogatory. So, what is going on? The woman is a Canaanite. To the disciples, then, she is not Jewish, but of another faith. Worse still, she is of a faith that is of mixed-weave, and cultic. This is one of the faiths despised by all good Jews – an old, established, faith, but one that is mixed in with more recent imports – Hellenistic, especially.

Dogs, of course, are not thoroughbreds. They rarely are. So, the derogatory remark from Jesus is pointed. Herself and her faith are 'dog-like'. These people and their religion are mixed breed. We also know that Jews sometimes called Gentiles 'dogs' for precisely this reason. They are impure. But Jews were pedigree.[11] Jesus' use of the word 'dog' implies 'the dogs outside (Judaism)'. But the woman is playfully insistent and uses the same word to mean 'the dogs inside'. She and Jesus both know that good Jews don't take the children's bread and throw it out to the dogs (*balein* means to throw outside). But the woman is clever, and relocates the dogs inside, under the table. This becomes an insider–outsider debate between Jesus and the woman, on the topic of dogs and bread. Jesus, remember, is for the outsiders, and making them insiders. The woman's daughter will be healed.

There are other reasons to pay attention to the reference to dogs. For some in neo-Canaanite religion, dogs were healing agents. They were a welcome presence in homes. Jews, in contrast, forbade them from homes, and kept them out of the synagogue courts. We know that in Canaanite tombs, dogs – or representatives of dogs – were buried with their owners. So, dogs are ambivalent creatures in Jesus' world. To some, friendly pets to be fed, and to others a metaphor signalling impurity. The central question of the Gospel reading is, therefore, do you feed the animals, or regard them as unclean?

These days, this is a church–identity debate too. Should the church be an inclusive body – 'inclusive' being often some kind of coded word for 'liberal' and 'accommodating'. Or should the church be 'exclusive' – a coded term for 'conservative', clear and excluding? I think that Jesus is for neither. He is, rather, for something much richer: *incorporation* – which is, of course, deeply linked to his own incarnation. Jesus is for the blend. The Kingdom of God project is not just for the Jews, but for all. It will incorporate Jew and Gentile; slave and free; male and female; saved and saintly, sick and sinner.

Jesus is an expression of God's heart for humanity. He is the body language of God. The Kingdom is for all. So, the ministry of Jesus will incorporate from the outset. It belongs in the alleys, not just the temple or synagogues. It will welcome Samaritans, not just Sadducees; Publicans, not just Pharisees. The wisdom of the body of Jesus – the Bread of Life – is teaching us about incorporation all the time: this is what the church is to be – a body that grafts into itself. It does not seek purity; it strives for perpetual incorporation, reconciling the world to Christ. We are to be one body, of one bread. Though we are many, we are one body, because we all share one bread (1 Cor. 10.17).

Interlude – A Break for Bread

It would be obvious, I suppose, to say that the earthly life and ministry of Jesus – and his advocacy and augmentation of the Kingdom of God – is the measure against which we judge the church. Jesus' ministry confounded his contemporaries, and it continues to disturb our sense of boundaries. He reaches out to the Samaritan woman; and tells stories about good Samaritans, much to the annoyance of his potentially loyal Judean audience. He embraces the widow, the lame, the ostracized, the deprived and despised, and the neglected. He befriends the sinners and sinned against. He takes his tea with tax collectors. The people Jesus reached out towards were excluded from the mainstream of society and faith. Jesus was no crowd-pleaser;

he was, rather, their confounder. Jesus was a disturber of crowds. He did not seek their praise or adulation. His actions often interrogate witnesses.

The Kingdom that Jesus preached, however, was more than just a creature of his adult imagination and inspirational prophetic vision. His childhood had taught him a thing or two about people, society and God. He grew up in occupied territories, so had seen the good and bad side of that coin – oppression traded off against organization. His childhood had included a sojourn in Egypt. And we know that by working in Joseph's trade – carpentry and building (Gk *tekton*) – he had, by living in Nazareth, been exposed to the nearby Roman settlement of Sepphoris. This was a Hellenized community of almost 30,000 in Jesus' childhood, compared to the population of Nazareth, which boasted a mere 300.

So, Nazareth was a dormitory village supplying labour to a much larger cosmopolitan community nearby. It would have been full of Gentiles of every kind. So, from an early age, Jesus would have been exposed to a world beyond his native parochial Judaism. The theatre at Sepphoris seated 5,000. It is almost certain that Joseph took Jesus. For Jesus, in his adult life, uses the Greek word 'hypocrite' quite a few times, which simply means 'actor' – one who is masked, and playing a part.

What is significant about this, I think, is this. Jesus' Kingdom of God project was, from the outset, supra-tribal. It reached out beyond Judaism to the Gentiles. Consider, for example, the feedings of the 5,000 and the 4,000. It is customary, in a lazy-liberal and rather reductive way, to suppose that the Gospel writers simply got their maths muddled, and were a bit confused about a single event. But in fact, there may be good reasons to regard these two miracles as being quite separate events. The feeding of the 5,000 takes place on the western banks of the Sea of Galilee. The region was almost entirely Jewish, and the 12 baskets of leftovers symbolize the 12 tribes of Israel.

What, then, of the feeding of the 4,000, and the seven baskets of leftovers? It is, after all, the same kind of territory where Jesus' healing of the Canaanite girl takes place. The theme of feeding and bread is shared. The event occurs on the eastern shores of the Sea of Galilee, and the region was almost entirely Gentile in composition (just as this healing happens in Tyre and Sidon).

The seven baskets of leftovers correspond to the seven Gentile regions of the time (Phoenicia, Samaria, Perea, Decapolis, Gaulanitis, Idumea and Philistia). Moreover, the baskets in the feeding of the 5,000 (*kophinos*) are smaller than those mentioned in the feeding of the 4,000 (*spuridi* – a basket big enough for a person, as with Paul in Acts 9.25). The point here is that the new manna from heaven will be distributed evenly, across all lands. There is plenty for all.

So of course, Jesus heals the Canaanite girl, just as he feeds the 4,000, a few verses later in Matthew's Gospel. Luke, we should note, does the same; the feeding of the 4,000 and the healing of the Canaanite girl are linked. The gospel of Christ is, in other words, radically inclusive: Jew, Greek, Gentile, slave, free – all shall be welcome in the Kingdom of God.

Final Reflection: Dogs at Play

Most people I know – especially clergy – have a list of the five best sermons they have ever heard; and the five worst. Because sometimes sermons just don't work; for example, never work with children and animals. I have seen some sermons go badly wrong with children, as they tend to speak the truth rather than give the right answers. I have seen a curate faint when he ate a daffodil in the pulpit. I can't remember the point of the sermon now, only the drama of trying to revive him. I have seen some unfortunate sermons involving pet dogs, cats, one tortoise and a snake. You can't make this up.

I recall attending a remote rural Welsh Anglican church some 40 years ago. I was youth-hostelling with friends, and we wanted a quiet, early service so we could spend the rest of the day walking. However, about five minutes before the service began, a large pack of uniformed Brownies descended – they had been camping nearby.

The priest, no doubt flustered by the dramatic and sudden shift in the age demographics of the congregation, attempted to improvise with a children's talk. So, he talked about his pet dog; and started to engage the young girls about their dog or favourite pet. Seconds later, one Brownie burst into tears. She missed her dog at camp. The tears and sobbing quickly went viral. Brown Owl took out one Brownie; then another; then some more. Soon, the whole Brownie pack was in meltdown. The leaders could barely cope; they ran out of tissues. This is still one of the fastest ways of emptying a church I have ever seen. The priest, in his sermon, was attempting to point out that 'I Love Dogs' is an anagram of 'God Is Love'. Fair enough. But the point was lost. The well-intentioned segue was lost on the Brownies. I suspect the sermon will never be used again.

But to call someone a dog is normally derogatory – unless the quality of the dog (determination, loyalty or enthusiasm come to mind) are being appealed to. So, there are some situations in which you can imagine the term being applied to humans in ways that are warm. For example, I don't believe in reincarnation. But if I did, and if I had to be reincarnated as an animal, I would come back as a St Bernard dog. I have my reasons. First, I'd like to be a saint, and this is as about close as I'll get. Second, I believe in searching for the lost. Third, everyone loves a good dog, so there is a chance of being both liked and gainfully employed, and you can rarely do both of these in the church – trust me on this. Finally, a rescue mission that involves a hip flask full of malt whisky can't be all that bad. Indeed, find or lose your victim, it still ends with a well-deserved drink. (Even though I am teetotal.)

In our house, we sometimes used to refer to bishops as 'Labradors' – loyal pets, enthusiastic and good-natured, easy to maintain, needing moderate exercise, and making good family dogs. They last about ten to twelve years if you treat them well (that's Labradors, not bishops). But they have a tendency to get overweight in later life (that's Labradors, not bishops). And then their eyesight goes too, and they get bad breath and are prone to wind (that's Labradors, not bishops). You can be more playful, still, if you choose. Is your archdeacon a bit of a

Rottweiler? What is it with those evangelicals: always behaving like energetic Border Collies, rounding everyone up? Or for that matter, Anglo-Catholics (a comparison to any category of toy dog will work here, usually – I jest, obviously).

I used to ask my theological students: 'Do you think Jesus got a surprise at the resurrection?' Some said; no, of course not; others surely covertly dismissed it as a trivial question. But my response was more mischievous. I said that as Jesus had lived by faith and died in faith, when he was raised from the dead it was most likely he got the most tremendous surprise. That is the life of faith. C. S. Lewis reflects this in *The Lion, the Witch and the Wardrobe*. The children discover that Aslan the lion comes back from the dead, having been killed by the witch. They ask him why, if he had the knowledge that this had to happen, he did not spare them the grief and sadness of his death. Aslan simply replies that although since ancient times this was always the hope it had never happened before. So, who could know for sure?

Every generation of Christians must face precisely the same challenge. How do we hold on to our valued identities and practices, yet be open to the surprises that God has in store? This beautiful healing story is a 'surprise encounter' between Jesus and someone who is not only a woman, and a true outsider, but who becomes an insider. So, we learn again that Jesus' mission is universal. It always was. Christ was born for all and died for all. There is no 'us' and 'them' any more: only one body, with one bread: a bread that needs sharing with all humanity.

Thy Kingdom Come:
Mission and Evangelism

Humility is nothing but truth, and pride is nothing but lying.
St Vincent de Paul

A few years ago, we crossed an unmarked line in the developmental life of the Church of England. The best-selling Report ever produced by the Church of England had been *Faith in the City* (Archbishop of Canterbury's Commission on Urban Priority Areas, 1985). Published in the eighties, it engaged seriously with the decay and despair in our inner-city communities. It changed, among other things, how we shaped the training of clergy. It shone a very public spotlight on our Urban Priority Areas (UPAs). It championed the poor. And for focusing on UPAs, the Report earned the opprobrium and scorn of the right-wing press.

But the more serious edge to the Report, and often missed, was that it marked out a particularly distinctive mode of theological reflection. For we might say that what *Faith in the City* represented was a kind of theology rooted in the Kingdom of God. One that put the people and the places they lived in before the needs and concerns of the church. The Report took seriously the fact that before the church took root as an institution, with its own needs and concerns to develop much later, the 'Jesus Project' began with preaching and proclaiming in word and deed, the Kingdom of God for all.

The moment of *Faith in the City* being the Church of England's best-selling Report, has, however, passed. The biggest-selling Church of England Report is now *Mission-Shaped Church*. For the uninitiated, this showcases forms of congregational life that appeal to homogenous groups, and are largely evangelical and evangelistic in character, appealing as they do to specific, identifiable and narrow interest groups (certain kinds of youth culture, etc.). These new emerging genres of church are usually apolitical in outlook, and often tend to be socially, politically and theologically conservative, as Robert Bellah has observed.

Thus, new forms of Fresh Expression promoted by the Church of England are normally careful to avoid anything that could be construed as theologically, politically or socially divisive. At the same time, these groups inhabit a social and theological construction of reality in which they believe themselves to be risk-takers and edgy. But they are usually anything but this. So, for example, we rarely learn of fresh expressions for the LGBTQ+ constituency. We rarely find any fresh expressions that focus on disabilities. Or, for that matter, on serious forms of exclusion from the mainstream of society. The fresh expression for asylum seekers would be an interesting kind of ecclesial gathering.

In all this, we must also remember that Jesus did not plant synagogues. Jesus did not grow synagogue congregations. Jesus did not advocate fresh expressions of synagogue. But Jesus did spend time with the marginalized and disenfranchised. Jesus did challenge prevailing religious structures and outlooks. Jesus did admit people to the Kingdom of God who were not Jewish. Often unconditionally. None were Christian at that point, or became so, needless to say.

To be sure, there are other kinds of ecclesial community that are advocated by *Mission-Shaped Church* and its spin-offs. So-called Pioneer ministry places clergy or lay ministers in communities or neighbourhoods that do not have access to a local church or are for other reasons excluded or marginalized from socio-ecclesial life. There are some remarkable testimonies of such ministry in places and among people that are 'off the grid'.

For example, I think of one pioneer minister who trained at Cuddesdon while I was Principal, who went on to minister in a working-class community with high historic unemployment, and exceptionally low literacy rates. In such a place, gathering people around a written liturgy was always unlikely to be the best recipe for ecclesial life. The 'church' that was planted in the community began with some basics – helping people to read for a start, which was itself a commendable act of socio-political intervention, empowering the community to engage with the social and civic services that were neglecting the community as a whole. This was good, earthy ministry.

The origins of our problem lie with the Decade of Evangelism. There was little discontent and much optimism when the 1988 Lambeth Conference passed a resolution approving a Decade of Evangelism. Each Province of the Communion was to develop plans for evangelism that led up the millennium. Most did, including the Church of England. But this marked a departure from *Faith in the City*. Because by the late 1980s, a new cultural turn in the Church of England was already underway. The Church of England was shifting to the right. Away from politics and *Faith in the City*, and towards charismatic evangelicalism. This lay emphasis on individual decisions for salvation; and healing as something individuals could claim and attain – despite poverty being the major cause of most illnesses across the globe.

Nonetheless, the late 1980s saw a significant ascendancy for evangelicals in the Church of England. And the Decade of Evangelism would be, to a considerable extent, a vehicle that gave them further prominence. Time, energies and resources were channelled in to making the Decade successful. With evangelism now firmly on the radar, this ought to have been the moment for evangelicals – the resident specialists in evangelistic theory and practice. But the Decade was an underwhelming affair. Church attendance and membership continued to decline. And as the more evangelical wing of the church asserted its overt brand of faith, the public quietly stepped back.

The problem – the legacy of this Decade, in effect – can be simply expressed. The Church of England – or at least its hierarchy – are stuck in *broadcast* mode. Like the proverbial Englishman abroad, they cannot make themselves understood in a world that increasingly finds the church incomprehensible. Especially in spheres such as sexuality, gender, equality, safeguarding, the exercise of power, the holding of authority and being open to accountability. But does the church perceive this? No. It just talks louder, hoping, somehow, it will be heard. It won't.

In all this, the church only seeks to make itself more appealing, and attractive to those who might join. Yet it rarely asks the same public why they don't join. It is like a business doing even more hard selling, with increasing desperation, but unwilling to ask the consumers why they aren't buying (if you don't research the reasons for your lack of 'footfall', it is no use blaming the stay-away consumers).

What is strange about this situation is that the drivers of the agenda are deeply concerned about mission and evangelism. So, they act out of the best of intentions. But the problem is that the underlying theology of mission and of the Holy Spirit – missiology and pneumatology – is deeply deficient. Let me explain more here. Expressive evangelistic campaigns tend to achieve very little. Even the Evangelical Alliance, in 1994, admitted that the main achievement of the Decade was to establish 'new levels of cooperation between the churches'. Hardly a great result. But as other writers in the field of missiology had known for years, what was compelling and credible was an authentic and humble church. One that listened deeply and lived its faith, faithfully and unassumingly, rather than brashly promoting its brand.

John V. Taylor's classic *The Go-Between God*, describes true mission as finding out what God is doing, and then trying to cooperate (Taylor, 1972). Evangelism, said Taylor, is primarily God's work; not a sacrificial effort on the part of the churches to appease God. So, let us turn to a Sufi mystic poet of the fourteenth century, who reminds us of the imperative of receptive partnership in mission. We do not just follow the desires of the flesh, body or latest church-fixation. We live by the Spirit and are therefore invited to always be open to the 'other', without whom we will not be complete. Or worse, may not encounter God. For God comes to us from without and within. Hafiz (1315–90) in his poem 'The Seed Cracked Open' puts it like this:

It used to be
That when I would wake in the morning
I could with confidence say,
'What am "I" going to
Do?'
That was before the seed
Cracked open.
Now Hafiz is certain:
There are two of us housed
In this body,
Doing the shopping together in the market and
Tickling each other
While fixing the evening's food.
Now when I awake
All the internal instruments play the same music:
'God, what love-mischief can "We" do
For the world
Today?'
(Hafiz, 1999, p. 35)

The poem echoes the words of Jesus in John's Gospel:

Very truly, I tell you, unless a grain of wheat falls into the
earth and dies, it remains just a single grain; but if it dies, it
bears much fruit. Those who love their life lose it, and those
who hate their life in this world will keep it for eternal life.
(John 12.24–25)

There is something in this about surrender to the other, and
to God. In all respects, we can learn nothing of love unless
we are vulnerable and open. We cannot receive and give love
by remaining closed. We cannot receive God, and offer God's
love, compassion and mercy, unless we are open. But having
received, we can begin to 'bear much fruit' (of the Spirit) and
pray with Hafiz: 'God, what love-mischief can "We" do/ For
the world/ Today?' The church needs to lose its 'I'; and learn
to see, love and receive the world as God does, and so embrace
the 'We'.

This *Missio Dei* is our traditional way, as a church, of understanding how God acts in the world, to reconcile all things to God through Christ. This recognizes that God is omnipresent, and can and does act in all creation – so not just within the recognized boundaries of ecclesial life (which are, in any case, like all borders, inherently contestable and marginal). There is ample scriptural warrant for thinking about the work of the Holy Spirit in just this way. The Jewish disciples, for example, 'discovering' that God is at work among the Gentiles – and that God had started something in those communities before any proactive mission had got underway.

The *Missio Dei* recognizes something crucial in God's ecology of mission. Namely, that God might choose to speak *from* the world *to* the church. The church, in other words, is not always God's starting point for conversion-related initiatives. Sometimes, God needs to convert the church, and can't do it from within. So, God works from without. The Holy Spirit is omnipresent, and at work ahead of the church, and outside it. The question, always, is can the church recognize this? And can the church *receive* what the Spirit is doing beyond its boundaries? And in the act of reception, be prepared to be reformed and renewed?

The answer from the churches to such questions – say on issues of gender, sexuality and equality – is frequently, 'no'. The church will not receive the progressive truth, justice and change that the world has undertaken and adopted. The church resists the change. It resists contemporary culture. It does not believe that the Holy Spirit could be at work independent of church leaders in our contemporary culture and could use that cultural change to reform and renew the church. So, the world, slowly but surely, backs away from the church, and leaves it to live in its own bubble of self-justifying rhetoric and self-shaping strategies. This gets the church nowhere, of course. Just further up the creek without a paddle. And as for evangelism, only the converted are left to be preached at.

We might point out the unevenness and contradictions of the church here. We are very willing and able to receive expertise from the private sector in spheres such as the reshaping of the financial funding formulas for clergy training. Or for providing a more 'incentivized' and 'targeted' approach to diocesan subsidies, that replaces a commitment of supplementation with entrepreneurial 'growth-led' bids that are then rewarded with 'grants'.

But the church can't seem to receive the wisdom of the world on equality legislation, safeguarding practices and protocols, the treatment of LGBTQ+ clergy and laity, and gender-related policies, which might include developing joined-up thinking on anything from parental leave to sexual harassment. Here, the church lags behind the world, locked into its own kind of bunker mentality. Meanwhile, a posse of ex-bankers and former civil servants are given free rein to reform the church in much the way they please.

We should be alive to the paradoxes here. As one commentator put it to me some while ago, it is as though the Christian Union have taken over the College Chapel. But the people now running the reformed services can't understand why all the people who used to come no longer attend. No amount of reorganization or enhanced evangelism can take away from the fact that the world experiences the way the church behaves as *alienating*. Pastorally, on the ground, we remain good, kind, authentic and engaged. It is the direction of travel and drive of the hierarchy that let us down.

So, all that said, any decent missiology would always critique the notion that the church or congregation is in possession of God's power, and then simply has a range of choices on how it reifies and dispenses such power. Any proper kingdom theology would try and reverse this perception. Can God not bring the gospel to the church from outside – and through agents and channels the church would not normally regard as pure, licensed or proper?

It is a simple question. What does God want to say to the church from the world? How can the church be open to and receive from what God is doing outside the church? Can it learn a lesson from its own exilic period?

This is the essence of Vincent Donovan's *Christianity Rediscovered* and the way in which the missionary was transformed by the Masai: those to be converted are the ones who do the converting (Donovan, 1982). I'm also reminded of two very contrasting approaches to mission witnessed 30 years ago, while I was training for ordination. Both were in a UPA in the North-East. The first project was evangelical, intense and focused on converting local people. The evangelical mission lasted just a few years – and then left: a lack of 'results'– stony ground, I daresay.

The second, Franciscan, arrived empty-handed. They drew in the community by asking them if they could help furnish the Brothers' bare flat. The locals obliged. The first item to arrive was a chair for the unfurnished sitting room – a passenger seat taken from a written-off Ford Capri. More bits of odd furniture arrived. A kettle was found. The Brothers rejoiced at every gift. The Franciscans still work there in the community. The Franciscans came to a community usually written off as a place of poverty and lack. Yet as the Brothers brought nothing, they affirmed their neighbours. They were able to encounter and encourage a community that was generous and resourceful. They liked to give, and they took pleasure and pride in looking after those less fortunate than themselves. That included the Brothers.

In return, the Brothers simply offered a ministry that listened, and only then helped. The Brothers made no assumptions about what the community lacked. They went in, expecting to find God's provision in what many would have described as a desert. They lived joyfully with their people and did not presume any lacking on the part of the community that they served. For the Franciscans, God was already dwelling there – long before they arrived. The same principles are at work in the beautiful novel by Dominique Lapierre, *The City of Joy*, set in the slums of Kolkata (Lapierre, 1986).

John Robinson, in his fine *The New Reformation* has this to say: 'We have got to relearn that "the house of God" is primarily the world in which God lives, not the contractor's hut set up in the grounds' (Robinson, 1965, p. 27). Put another way, the church was only ever meant to be the constructor's hut on God's building site, which is the world (or if preferred, substitute 'Kingdom of God' for 'world'). The church is not God's main project. The world is. So, let me give two examples of what this looks like in terms of mission and ministry. The first is reactive; the second proactive. Both examples remind us that the church must listen if it wishes to speak; silent if it wishes to proclaim.

The first of these examples has the same roots (trauma) that gave birth to the Samaritans under Chad Varah. As a curate in the city of Lincoln in 1935, he had taken the funeral of a girl who had killed herself. In 1953, he founded the Samaritans in the crypt of his London church, attributing the girl's death – whom he did not know – as the seed that gave birth to this extraordinary new work. A ministry, effectively, that transcended the church.

In a similar vein, the suicide of a 14-year-old girl in 2014 also caused a change in direction for ministry. This time, the girl had taken her life because she feared she might be gay. But she was a member of a prominent evangelical Church of England congregation in Didsbury, Manchester. She believed that to be a lesbian was wrong. The teaching of the church said so. Unable to cope with the guilt, her feelings, and her sense that she would face condemnation – in this life, or the next – she took her own life.

The suicide had a significant impact on the congregation. The girl had been a prominent member of the youth group. But in the congregational soul-searching that followed in the wake of the suicide, the church began to change. It moved from being benignly homophobic to being proactively inclusive. Some established members of this evangelical church therefore left. But new people came, including groups and individuals who had never felt they could be welcomed at a church such as this. The congregation grew, even though it had moved from being evangelical to inclusive. The exilic lesson was learned. This church could now receive from the community around it, and because of its receptiveness and hospitality, it began to grow. Differently. Better?

My second illustration comes from Australia and is an example of some extraordinary progressive pastoral ministry.

Like many clergy, the rector of this parish was more than used to being asked by new parents who had little or no relation to the church, if they would nonetheless baptize their child. Most clergy would respond to this request with encouragement and catechesis. The clergy would normally insist on stipulating a course of Christian instruction for the parents – sometimes lasting months. Many clergy would also insist that the baptism took place in the context of a normal act of worship, to enculturate the parents, godparents, wider family and friends into the ways of faith.

But not this priest. The rector took a different view, and let the parents choose the time for the baptism to begin with – a Saturday, or even a Sunday afternoon, and a 'private' ceremony was countenanced. Frequently, this was the preferred option, as it suited families with their dispersed range of relatives. Then the rector, in seeing the parents, would go further. To begin with, he handed over a copy of the Bible and a hymn book, and invited the couple to keep these copies, but to choose a hymn and Bible reading for their service. He made it clear too that they could also use other songs and readings as supplements – but they were to choose a hymn and Bible reading that spoke to the couple about what God meant to them in the birth of this child. So far, so good.

Then he added this. The couple were to choose between themselves, or nominate someone else from the wider family, a person to give the short homily that accompanies the baptism. Yes, the family were going to provide the preacher. But the sermon was a simple thing explained the rector, and need cover only three things. First, what were their family values? What did this family stand for, and what mattered to them as virtues? Second, how were the family and friends attending the baptism proposing to raise this child in accordance with those values? And third, as they had chosen the hymn and Bible reading, how did the rookie preacher think God was going to be involved in this family now, and helping with the raising of this child? How would they collectively respond to God's commitment to this child in baptism? As the rector reported, no family ever failed to produce a riveting, rich sermon and testimony to

God's grace and providence. They became conduits of God's grace; unwitting ambassadors of the gospel message.

What is the lesson here? Instead of the church preaching *at* the family, hoping a few seeds would take root – somehow – the rector got the family to preach to themselves. The result was that most of the seeds at least germinated. And many took root. As an exercise in evangelism this was clearly far more effective. And, of course, it proceeds from a far more trusting, generous-orthodox pneumatology and missiology.

In this example, the church places itself in a humble position where it receives the gospel from the world. It is a risk but it does not fatally fall for the flaw that always assumes the church possesses the truth, and needs to pester the world with it. Or is permanently casting itself in the role of broadcaster to an indifferent audience. This approach to evangelism strikes an entirely different note. Most clergy would feel obliged to preach at the baptism and to the gathering. The rector's initiative, however, ensured that the family remembered the homily for a very long time: every word. They had preached it.

In a similar vein, the same rector used to hold a monthly Evensong, and invite local community leaders, heads of local business, charities, or other members of the community, to preach. The same formula was followed. A Bible and hymn book handed over to the unsuspecting (often non-religious, or non-observant individual), inviting them to pick a hymn and Bible passage, and then talk to the congregation – and any of their own friends or colleagues who happened to be invited to come along – about what their work meant to the town, how it built up community values, contributed to wider society, and helped and supported others. As the rector said, it was the easiest way to get several dozen new people into church every month. They simply could not contain their curiosity at what one of their own might say from the pulpit about values, hope and faith. And God. No one declined the invitation. And all had something to say about the good news for the community. God spoke through each preacher.

(A note to anxious clergy at this point. Yes, the rector always had a spare homily just in case. And yes, those preaching at a baptism or one of the Evensong's often checked their text with the rector beforehand – only natural when it is your first time preaching in front of friends, family and colleagues.)

If we started with a theology of evangelism rooted in the values of the Kingdom of God and *Missio Dei*, the churches would spend much more time listening, and less time talking. More time receiving from the world, and less time pumping out propaganda. But I wonder, sometimes, if church leaders really do trust God, and genuinely believe in the omnipresent power of the Holy Spirit abroad in mission? Our leaders don't talk and behave as though they do believe this. They seem to think it all depends on them. They sound, all too often, like sacred custodians of a tribal deity in a remote village. Their God is small and tame; but it is *their* god. But all transcendence has been thoroughly domesticated.

Too often, our church leaders behave as though all that matters is the church. Sometimes, the reputation and safeguarding of the church can be put before justice, integrity and truth. Even before compassion. To borrow from Pope Francis, the church is not a 'custom house' – it is a field hospital. It exists not for the perfect, but for sinners. God's mercy extends far beyond the church. Our leaders, though, conservative as they are, create a kind of 'marsh' on areas such as safeguarding, gender and sexuality, only hampering progress. Their world is one of determined resistance, born of fearful or hardened hearts, content with the empty rhetoric of (spiritual) window dressing, typical of those who say they are ready for change, but want everything to remain as before.

Yet tradition is not an unchangeable bank account. It is the doctrine of going forward. The essential does not change; but it grows and develops. How does it grow and develop? It grows like a person – through dialogue – dialogue with ourselves, and dialogue with the world around us. If we are not engaged in dialogue, we are not able to grow. The church will stand still. It will remain small. We will eventually be dwarfed by the world around us. People will speak over our heads.

'Jesus is the answer, what was your question?' would be a fair characterization of our current evangelistic approach as a national church. If our church leaders think they do have all the answers, behaving like defensive omnicompetent rulers, I doubt we will sound as though we are genuinely interested in the concerns and questions that people may have. If the Church of England really wants to recover some vision for national mission, and something of the urgency of evangelism, then there is only one thing to do to begin with. Nothing.

Yes, nothing. Just be still. And then learn to listen to the world around. Then we might hear what the actual cares and concerns of our communities are. Then we might begin to discern where God is already at work. Then we might receive from these communities what God would have this church become. Then we might see 'Thy Kingdom Come'.

Jesus and the Self-Emptying Church

'Thank you' is the best prayer that anyone could say. I say that one a lot. 'Thank you' expresses extreme gratitude, humility, understanding ...
Alice Walker

Even before the Covid-19 pandemic began, global citizens faced a dizzying list of crises, which I have previously listed: including climate change with myriad human causes, desperate inequalities, unsustainable ways of living, and countless obstacles to solving these problems with the urgency they need. Thus far this century, our churches have struggled with these agendas. In an age when we needed leaders in the church to address the considerable challenges in our communities and nations, many denominations have found themselves distracted, and locked into their own insular battles for identity and survival. Disagreements have raged and ranged over issues such as sexuality and gender, or even involved internecine battles for resources. The world has looked on, aghast at our blinkered blundering.

However, recent events have meant there is no longer a hiding place left for the churches. We have arrived at a new threshold in the twenty-first century; one I described as a new 'BC' and 'AC' – Before Coronavirus and After Coronavirus. Profound and searching questions are bound to be asked of those bodies that have been weighed and found wanting during these current crises. Equally, scrutiny will also turn to those institutions and bodies that have proved to be essential, good and generative in these crises – publicly useful, providing care and compassion, leadership and community service. Institutions embodying generosity, sacrifice and solidarity will continue to take a lead, and rightly so.

Churches may have done well to deliver engaging worship 'remotely' and developed on-line networks for pastoral care and prayer. However, in the emerging era, it is doubtful that many Diocesan Mission Statements will be worth the flip-chart sheets, masses of Post-it notes and PowerPoint presentations they were written on. It is sobering to note that all it took to blow the myths and mirages of 'vision statements' and 'growth targets' out of the water was a virus that is smaller than the size of a pinprick. Tiny things can make a substantial difference.

Quite suddenly, our commitments to dozens, even hundreds of new congregations to be 'planted' across Dioceses, and thousands of new disciples to be 'developed' seem less important, and even irrelevant. Such rhetoric has pervaded and peppered the set-piece speeches of our church leaders for decades. Such hypothetical constructions of reality have done little to help hard-pressed clergy and congregations; and done much to demoralize and induce guilt. The churches are about to enter a new era of crisis, as our attention turns to the vast numbers of bereaved, lonely and jobless. Fantasies and fetishes of growth will have little place in this soon-to-be-emerging world, that will have already divested itself of delusional voices and visions promoting endless progression.

Crises are, of course, opportunities. So, can a more open church emerge out of the Covid-19 crisis? Can we imagine a context in which congregations and leaders don't try a return to peddling answers to questions that people are not actually asking? A church that listens, and instead of constantly being stuck in 'broadcast mode', becomes more genuine and perceptive in 'reception mode'?

I believe we can. But this means discarding a model of the church that is still seeking its own pre-eminence in society – putting the church back, somehow, in the positional status some think it still deserves. In many respects, by keeping our churches shut during the pandemic crisis, and confining our clergy to home, church went 'private', when it most needed to be public. Yet I dare to live in hope. And that hope is that we relearn what it is to be a humble church, led by leaders who are immersed in humility, and so grounded in listening first, rather than proclaiming and pontificating. A key to this is the discovery – or rather, recovery – of a 'kenotic ecclesiology'.[12] Emma Percy's poem, 'Another Economy', expresses this:

> I have found that there is a different economy
> Whose currency is
> Love and kindness
> Faithfulness and prayer
> Generosity and integrity.
> When these virtues are practised
> Deposits are made and investments accrued.
> So, when the world turns harsh
> And desolation beckons,
> I find I am rich.
> And I can draw on this wealth
> Providing me with
> Friendship and kindness
> Prayers and blessings
> Fortitude and strength.
> (Percy, 'Another Economy', 2019)

Humility as Grounding

Humility is the quality of being humble. But in our person-centred-fulfilment-therapeutically-attuned culture, we often conflate humility with humiliation. We assume low self-regard and unworthiness to be debasing. Yet in religion, the charism of humility is rooted in perspective and submission – and being 'un-salved': a liberation from consciousness of the self; a form of temperance that is neither having pride (or haughtiness) nor indulging in self-deprecation. Granted, this has to be carefully calibrated for particular contexts. Perspectives from liberation and feminist theology, for example, or those theologies that represent and advocate 'protected characteristics' (sexuality, disability, race, age, religion, etc.) will quite rightly draw our attention to the inequalities in power dynamics that can emerge and become abusive. When humility is imposed on people – directly or indirectly through force or expectation – it can become a form of subjugation that is little more than a code for 'submission'.

To be clear, the imposition of humility by those in power as a means of expediting domination over others is not what we are concerned with here. Rather, we are concerned with the true humility that comes from a deep inner self-confidence and attends to the needs of and the valuing of others. The humble person is not preoccupied with themselves, but rather occupied with the needs of others. Humiliation, in contrast, is imposed on us externally, and it frequently shames us.

True humility is almost unattainable, and real humiliation undesirable. Yet both terms are linked to the words humus and hubris. 'Humus' means being earthed, and the humble person is a grounded person: surer of their being, so not above themselves – and knowing they are not above others, no matter what giftedness, rank, or status they hold. 'Hubris', in contrast, is self-inflated, puffed-up self-perception; and it lacks grounded-ness. Grounding is fundamental, as Justine Allain-Chapman notes:

> Humility is the quality that ... all mature Christians grow into; a quality where a deep sense of inner dignity and value is palpable to others and brings them solace, it is a fruit of the Spirit, sometimes translated as 'gentleness'. It can be mis-understood as a false modesty of doing yourself down and as such can be quite manipulative, in refusing to allow others to express gratitude or admiration, for example. Humble people are grounded (which means lowly, on the ground or earth). They are secure in themselves and in touch with their own vulnerability as human beings but also fully aware of their strengths. (Allain-Chapman, 2018, p. 111)

Jesus tells us that 'all who exalt themselves will be humbled, and all who humble themselves will be exalted' (Matt. 23.12). The Letter of James (4.6) reminds us that 'God opposes the proud, but gives grace to the humble.' An account in John 13 recalls a night when Jesus washed the feet of his disciples, and in so doing, elected to serve, humbling himself.

In one of the most remarkable theological meditations of relatively recent years, Daniel Hardy and David Ford reflect on how the ecology of praise, joy and laughter is an essential component in the facing of evil, suffering and death (Hardy and Ford, 1984). They highlight the inadequacy of stoicism and call for a deeper theological response to the wickedness, malice and crises that individuals and communities may face. They argue that joy and praise – rooted in our acknowledge-ment of the overwhelming abundance of God – can help us to face the darkness that threatens to envelop us, and address it with a different perspective. This means anticipating the flow of the Spirit of God in our lives, and uniquely embodied in the life of Jesus, which expresses the ultimate overflow of praise to God, and the most manifest intensification of the good news of the Kingdom. Jesus is the Verb of God.

The self-conscious kenosis of Christ anticipates this in the way of the cross. But 'self-emptying' here is not a resigned stoicism. It continues to be, in Jesus, a journey of praising, knowing and joy; but which also faces evil and suffering. Golgotha is not for himself; it is for us. It is a kind of surrender. But not of stoicism and self-resignation; it is a surrender to God, into whose hands Jesus commits himself. The cross is therefore also an act of will and resistance too, for it refuses to abandon hope in the face of torture, agony, isolation and death.

So Hardy and Ford remind us that while patience, endurance and bravery are all important (in discipleship and leadership), this stoicism will not be enough as a proper theological response to the forces of evil that are sometimes faced, and the suffering that results. Daringly, they argue that stoicism can prevent us from really facing the intensification of shame that sometimes grips institutions and communities, causing them to transfer their blame to others. Here, they sagely suggest, 'only joy can creatively oppose evil in all its perversion of both order and non-order; stoicism at best contains it, resists it and maintains order and dignity in the face of it' (p. 141).

Therefore, they argue, it is only the overwhelming abundance of God – and the proper response of joy and praise to this – that can truly address the darkness that threatens to envelop. To enter an understanding of God's ecology is to see that in God, there is no darkness or light, but only one equal light. Thus, even demanding difficulty and apparent loss can be transfigured. This requires, however, a kind of faith, hope and trust for what will be, and for what is: who we are already before God. It is this kind of kenosis – a self-emptying in order to be filled with the joy of the Spirit, and the overwhelming abundance of God – that makes the way of servant leadership so demanding, and yet so very liberating. It is a different kind of existence to that of stoicism.[13]

Kenotic Ecclesiology and Church Leadership

In view of this, where might we locate a Christian theology of humble church leadership? To be sure, no leader is remotely like Jesus, or ever could be. But are there lessons in his being that we might learn from? Here, I turn to kenosis – a term that generally refers to the 'self-emptying' of Christ and is an aspect of the doctrine of the incarnation. It is expressed most succinctly in the (so-called) 'Christological Hymn' from Paul's letter to the Philippians 2.6–11:

> Christ Jesus, who, though he was in the form of God,
> did not regard equality with God
> as something to be exploited,
> but emptied himself,
> taking the form of a slave,
> being born in human likeness.
> And being found in human form, he humbled himself
> and became obedient to the point of death –
> even death on a cross.
> Therefore God also highly exalted him
> and gave him the name
> that is above every name,
> so that at the name of Jesus

every knee should bend,
in heaven and on earth and under the earth,
and every tongue should confess
that Jesus Christ is Lord,
to the glory of God the Father.

Here we are faced with an incomparable sense of God's crea-tive restraint that ends in praise. Indeed, this call to humility and hope is rooted in the overwhelming abundance of God. The Hymn follows on from a meditative soliloquy from Paul on the nature of character in Christian leadership (Phil. 2.1–5):

> If then there is any encouragement in Christ, any consolation from love, any sharing in the Spirit, any compassion and sympathy, make my joy complete: be of the same mind, having the same love, being in full accord and of one mind. Do nothing from selfish ambition or conceit, but in humility regard others as better than yourselves. Let each of you look not to your own interests, but to the interests of others. Let the same mind be in you that was in Christ Jesus.

Theological reflection of this kind would have resonance, cen-turies later, in the *Rule of Benedict* (instructing the abbot), *Gregory's Pastoral Letter* (instructing bishops), right the way through to Robert Greenleaf's more modern meditative dis-course of servant leadership (Greenleaf, 1991).

Churches are to be, therefore, as Stanley Hauerwas notes, 'communities of character' (Hauerwas, 2013). In such com-munities, people are being disciplined by the grace of God into the new life that God, in Christ, has claimed them for. Such communities are consciously renewed by the salvific action of God in Christ. This is kenotic in character. It is by following the one who 'emptied himself', that one discovers the foundation for the charism of humility, and the space for joy in others, and in God. Donald MacKinnon, commenting on the theology of Donald Baillie, states that 'in Christ God is revealed as submitting himself to the very substance of human life, in its inexorable finitude, in its precarious ambiguity, in its movement to despair' (MacKinnon, 1993, p. 56).

Correspondingly, those notions of omnipotence and omniscience – and that so afflict our ecclesiology and church leaders – are transformed by kenosis. Jesus becomes the obedient one. He is the one who becomes 'obedient unto death' – even when that death is utterly unjust. This obedience must mean that the crucifixion is real; for in his humanity, Jesus must embody it all in its fullness – including despair. This, argues MacKinnon, leads the church to living 'an exposed life; it is to be stripped of the kind of security that tradition, whether ecclesiological or institutional, easily bestows' (MacKinnon, 1969, p. 34).

So, rather than attending to security and safety, underpinned by a fear of death, humiliation and annihilation, the church is asked to 'let go and let God'. This means there is a potential unfaithfulness to the gospel when opposing any enemy or external threat that poses a risk to its very existence. As MacKinnon further notes, when the Christian God is endowed with the attributes of a human Caesar, the church takes on the image of a 'transcendent Caesar' rather than the more fundamentally disruptive calling of embodying the 'vulnerable Nazarene'. For MacKinnon:

> From Christ there issues a continually repeated question, and his Church is his authentic servant only in so far as it allows that interrogation to continue. It is always easier to escape its remorseless probing: to take refuge in the security of a sharply defined orthodoxy, or to blur the riddling quality of its disturbing challenge by conformity to the standards of the age. (MacKinnon and Kirkland, 2011, p. 264)

What this means in practice is that Christians are incorporated into Christ's perpetual oblation. Christians are participative in the life of Christ, and in our self-emptying, wilful descent, and conscious path of humility, we are bound to an ecology of obedience rather than one of mere self-preserving resistance (Williams, 2018). In effect, kenotic Christology leads us to kenotic ecclesiology: we become the body of Christ when we participate more fully in the reality of Jesus' incarnation.

This, I should say, does not call the church, or individuals or groups within the church, to a life of passive acceptance or stoicism. It invites us to contemplate the formation and habitation of the character of community or individual that is being afflicted or persecuted. But here we are not asked to model weakness, but *meekness*. There is a paradox at the heart of kenosis. It is not a weary resignation in the face of the malign forces of fate. It is, rather, an act of determination and resolve; an exercise of deep power from within that chooses – in the example of God in Christ – to limit power and knowledge, but not to limit love, hope, joy and peace. The path of leadership will be one of obedience, accepting that a conscious and deep form of humility will no longer privilege power and knowledge. Rather, these will be set aside in a continuous, wilful and generative life of humility, that will place others above the self.

Such self-limiting of power and knowledge allows love to both cover and hold those who need it most. Indeed, I think many parents will understand something of this. What the child needs to experience is a parent with *some* power and *some* knowledge; but not too much, or else growth and individuation will be stifled. But this can only be fixed within a paradigm of unconditional love, that seeks to sustain and serve the ones we seek to nurture, and then set free.[14] And only love can do this. As it frees, it binds us. There can be something apophatic about Christ's way of leadership: humility preferred to privilege (Williams, 2018b).

Kenotic leadership then, is a form of being that does not allow negativity to germinate. The self-emptying paradigm that is exemplified in Jesus leads to a humble kind of leadership that serves others and befriends all, rather than merely seeing people as potential converts. As Chloe Lynch argues, the kenotic is a form of extraordinary self-giving friendship that Jesus models with his disciples, and with a wider public (Lynch, 2019). His meekness is magisterial. The one who reigns does so from a tree; his crown is made of thorns.

Conclusion

The concept of a kenotic ecclesiology will be something to reflect upon in the coming years. However, there are two senses in which one could understand the term 'self-emptying church'. A genuinely kenotic ecclesiology might lead to a church that models the humility of Jesus and pays little regard to itself. It will not 'cling' to its status, but empty itself, taking the form of a servant. It will feed the poor and shelter the homeless. It will put energy and resources into foodbanks and credit unions. It will pray and give, but not count the cost.

The other kind of 'self-emptying church' will fret about its size and following. It will embark upon endless recruitment drives. It will talk-up its status, boast about its increases, and be consumed by its own self-importance. It will constantly refrain mantras from texts drawn from selected various 'grammars of growth', reciting them excitedly in sepulchred echo chambers.

There are enormous numbers of books available on Christian leadership, and an equally large number of books on how to grow the church. Some of these are rich in biblical and spiritual reflection. Others seek to import a wealth of insight from secular and commercial spheres or can be quite plainly pragmatic. While the approaches taken in such books have some merit, few have much depth of discernment. In such contexts, leadership – and the possibility of a 'growing church' – are often presented as something all-too-easily attainable: it merely requires more resources, skills, and vision.

Church leadership and church growth is, however, seldom simple. The leadership requires high levels of emotional, ecclesial, educational and spiritual intelligence: a wisdom, that fits and fosters the institution, and the context in which that institution operates and serves. The realization of church growth often requires due attention and respect for the environment in which the church is situated. What grows a church in one context may not work in another. Or, worse, cause it to decline. As Tim Spector (2020) points out in relation to food, many 'fad' diets are based on myths and non-existent averages. One person can do well counting calories. For another, it will make little difference – ever. Some people are healthier on low-fat diets; some will not benefit at all; and some will actually incur some health-related detriment. As for the differences in our bodies – size, shape, metabolism, and so forth – so it is for more complex social bodies too, like churches. Just as 'one-size-fits-all' growth strategies will always promise more than they deliver, and impute more guilt than encouragement, so it is with what churches consume, and are equally consumed by.

So, spiritual leadership requires a combination of discernment, care, attentiveness, wisdom, will, direction and faithfulness. What makes and forms leaders in ecclesial contexts will be their reservoirs of compassion and empathy; a capacity to operate paternally and maternally; suppleness and firmness; forgiveness and discipline. Leaders see God at work through their own weaknesses and deficiencies, and not just the apparent strengths and attributes that they and others may cherish. Revitalizing the church requires our living as people to be rooted in the love God shows us in Christ, and asks us to hold this world of ours, that is often riven by strife and enmity. Paul daringly writes:

> Rejoice in hope, be patient in suffering, persevere in prayer ... Bless those who persecute you; bless and do not curse them ... do not be haughty, but associate with the lowly; do not claim to be wiser than you are. Do not repay anyone evil for evil ... if your enemies are hungry, feed them; if they are thirsty, give them something to drink ... do not be overcome by evil, but overcome evil with good. (Rom. 12.12–21)

God dwells in the world, and the task of the church is to be the architect and agent of what God is seeking to rebuild, restore and recreate – the coming Kingdom. Helping to bring about the Kingdom of God *is* Christian faith. We are not called to be devoted members of the Church Preservation Society (good work though such bodies undoubtedly do for our heritage and spirituality). For Christians, Jesus is the body language of God. He sees the unseen; hears the unheard; speaks for the mute and marginalized; touches the untouchable. The incarnation reconciled the gap between humanity and divinity. The incarnation, death and resurrection of Jesus was rooted in kenosis and service. In Christ, there is no longer 'social distance' between us and God. God chose to dwell with us in Christ in order that we might be one with another, and one with God. God accomplished this through the kenosis of Christ.

Calling for leaders who can help us model churches on the self-emptying of Jesus will probably not win that many advocates from among our current ecclesial hierarchies. Nonetheless, I hope and pray for a new kind of humble, listening church to emerge from our post-pandemic world. One that is openly grounded, unambiguously loving, and attentive to all. One less absorbed by congregational survival or growth, and more focused on public service. One less preoccupied with its own self-esteem, and more fully occupied with the God who chose to dwell among us as one of us, and lead as a servant. One that is no longer self-fulfilling, but rather, through following Jesus, becomes self-emptying. In other words, nothing less than the body of Christ for our emerging post-pandemic age: something self-giving, self-sacrificing, open, grounded, humble and loving.

Endings: Lowly, Living, Loving

One cannot be humble and aware of oneself at the same time.
Madeleine L'Engle

Making a humble pie requires some cooking skills and perhaps a recipe, or at least some idea of what you are doing in the kitchen. But our essential ingredients are always the same – common and base. As we noted at the beginning, these are the ingredients that Jesus chose to work with to advance the message of the Kingdom of God, and begin the initiative we now refer to as the church. God's wisdom does create things with the ingredients that the world discounts, disregards and despises. As Paul reminds us (1 Cor. 1.27–29), 'God chose what is foolish in the world to shame the wise; God chose what is weak in the world to shame the strong. God chose what is low and despised in the world, things that are not, to reduce to nothing things that are, so that no one might boast in the presence of God'. Peter exhorts the early church like this: 'all of you must clothe yourselves with humility in your dealings with one another, for "God opposes the proud, but gives grace to the humble"' (1 Peter 5.5; see also James 4.6).

Taking on the vocation of humility – being 'clothed' with humility, indeed – through prayer and community ought to lead the church to freedom, openness and discovery. We are too often split between elitism and nihilism. The church oscillates between a misplaced confidence – we know all the answers, and don't need help from the outside world – on the one hand, and on the other, the traditions and practices of the past and present need consigning to the wilderness – let us try something new. The elitism is sceptical of new initiatives; the nihilism presumes we can only be saved by these new initiatives.

Yet there is nothing new about the church. It is always being reformed from within and without, and for this reason alone, it needs to be a receptive body – the social skin of the world – that is both communicative and receptive, responsive and resilient, firm yet supple. Like any body-politic in society, it must breathe and eat, and listen and learn, as well as speak and teach. The radical nature of the church lies in following the example of its founder, Jesus, who was both receptive and responsive. To be the body of Christ today means the church being more of a field hospital than a customs house: we are here to tend and care, not to tax and control.

If one has to imagine the paradox of fullness and emptiness simultaneously, then the paradox is rooted in the person of Jesus. On the one hand, 'full of grace and truth' (John 1), and on the other 'emptied of all' (Phil. 2). As W. H. Vanstone noted, the church today requires 'divestment' to be embodied. We want it to be filled, because our security so often lies in fullness. Who wants an emptiness that leaves us feeling small, vulnerable and humble? And yet it is at this moment that we are enveloped, enfolded in love and filled. Vanstone reminds us, the measureless voids are the spaces where the Spirit broods; the wilderness and desert are where God finds us; and it is beyond the margins where there is seemingly nothing and no one, that Jesus seeks and finds the lost. As Vanstone notes, this is the calling of the church for today:

> The Church is not 'the cause which the Church serves' or 'the spirit in which the Church lives'; the Church is the service of that cause and the actualization of that spirit in words spoken, in bodies in a certain place or posture … Here, at this level of concrete actuality is the response of recognition to the love of God. (Vanstone, 1977)

Lowly

The grounding of the incarnation lies in God choosing to become flesh – Jesus dwelling among us, and sharing our life with all its pain, uncertainty and anxiety, as well as hope, joy and love. In Bethlehem 2,000 years ago, God enters history in an entirely new, decisive way – yet it is done in the midst of squalor, birth, potential shame (Joseph is not the father) and on a journey that no one is exempt from, as the military and political masters of the region have decreed that there will be a census. Christmas cards depicting nativity scenes, however, are often deceptive. Most portrayals of Jesus' birth offer clean-swept stables, fresh straw, unvarnished oak and pine, and thick woollen shawls and throws, that sanitize and romanticize poverty; a country-style birth straight from the glossy pages of an up-market home furnishing catalogue. The truth is probably more surprising; Jesus was surrounded by animals and filth, with nought for company save a few rough shepherds. Jesus, it appears, was born poor – a working class lad from Nazareth, born in Bethlehem, but who made good.

Yet closer attention to the Gospels reveals another side to Jesus which is much more comfortable – even middle class. Jesus was only born in a stable because the hotels were fully booked. Mary and Joseph could afford bed and breakfast, so they were clearly not that poor. They had their own transport too (granted only 1 bhp). Moreover, when the wise men came to visit, they brought quite expensive gifts – gold, frankincense and myrrh have never been cheap. What does one suppose Jesus' parents did with these gifts? Was it a case of (a) can't believe our luck – store away for a rainy day (b) straight to the pawnbrokers, or (c) they'll go nicely on the mantelpiece, next to those other ornaments our relatives picked up from their holiday in Persia?

Portraiture of Jesus has hidden his true class origins to our detriment. It is actually probably quite important that we see Jesus as being born into a relatively comfortable strata of society. Consider the evidence. Mary and Joseph had the money to flee to Egypt and live abroad for a few years, in order to escape Herod's wrath. Generally, the poor do not have these resources at their disposal. Carpentry was more of a skilled building industry than a basic utility trade: wood was fundamental to the structure of most housing. The holy family could afford a pilgrimage or two, and in Luke's Gospel were enjoying it so much that they didn't even notice that Jesus was missing. Jesus was educated; well educated, in fact. There were no comprehensive schools in Nazareth, but Jesus had the financial resources to learn to read and write, and trained as a rabbi. Even at his death, he owned an expensive seamless robe, and his body was smuggled away by a foreign merchant to be given a 'decent' burial.

Further support for this thesis comes, strangely enough, from Eusebius' *Ecclesiastical History, Book III:20*. The writer, quoting a first-century source, says that the descendants of Jesus' family were rounded up during a persecution, with a view to their land being confiscated. Eusebius tells us that 'they had enough to be self-sufficient'. Not really wealthy, but certainly comfortable.

So, if Jesus was from a good, Jewish, middle-class background, what are the implications for Christians? Ironically, they are far more disturbing than if he had been born poor. It would appear that Jesus, in his ministry, turned his back on his class roots, and that he chose poverty. 'Blessed are the poor: for theirs is the Kingdom of Heaven.' Jesus believed a rich man would struggle to gain entry into heaven; he assumed the poor would be there by right. Jesus made friends among the poor – sinners, prostitutes, the mentally ill, widows – and he invariably challenged the wealthy over their pride and complacency. The Christian paradigm, in Jesus at least, is 'sell all you have', 'take no gold and silver for the journey', and always bless the beggar, the homeless and the hungry. It's radical stuff, and its anti-bourgeois. No wonder he got on people's nerves.

The early Christian Socialists – such as F. D. Maurice, Stewart Headlam and John Ludlow understood – understood that God discriminated for the poor, and shared something of the radical nature of Jesus' chosen social incarnation. They worked with Chartists, radicals, and other organizations to bring justice for the working class. They argued for universal suffrage, set up colleges and co-operatives, and laboured for the labourer. It was a costly agenda: Maurice lost a Chair in Theology at King's College, London, for his trouble. Yet he never lost the imperative: the poor were God's cause, and a truly Socialist society would never abandon them.

What is interesting about the lowliness of Jesus is that it does not just involve 'self-emptying', and the kind of humility we might ordinarily associate with a kind of personal piety. Jesus' 'kenosis' emptied his wallet (so to speak), and it is hardly surprising that on several occasions when he mentioned purses (for example, Luke 10.4; 12.33; 22.35 and Matt. 10.9) his disciples must have winced at the call to a lowly, humble life. For Jesus, this meant losing the things we have become dependent upon, in order to encounter the grace of dependency on God. So, Jesus leaves his friends and family too. He tells his disciples to do the same in Luke 14.26 and Matthew 19.29. The Kin-dom of God was to be a new kind of order, in which bonds were based on love of neighbour, stranger and even enemy. Jesus forsook the comforts of family life to develop spiritual relationships that replaced the maternal, paternal and filial.

Then, as now, this offended friends and family alike, and even Jesus' own family complain about the company he now seems to prefer keeping (Matt. 12.46–50). In family life even today, you may occasionally hear some aggrieved family member uttering the proverb, 'Blood is thicker than water'. Some think it is biblical, although like, 'God helps those who help themselves', the phrase is pseudo-scriptural. The actual proverb hails from medieval English, and means that familial bonds will always be stronger than bonds of friendship or love.

Yet the proverb has its own mixed parentage, and is not what it seems on closer inspection. The equivalent medieval Arab proverb is 'Blood is thicker than (mother's) milk', which conveys the idea that any two children nourished at the same breast are called 'sucking brothers' or 'milk-brothers'. So, although their ties are close and strong, the blood relative – the children of the covenant – are closer than those who are merely weaned together.

More recently, just over a century ago, Aldous Huxley's *Ninth Philosopher's Song* (1920) affirmed the English medieval proverb, but added 'But water's wider, thank the Lord, than blood'. Other commentators have argued that the 'water' is the water of the womb – the semiotic fluid that surrounds a child before it is born – and so the blood of the covenant is more binding than actual family ties.

In nativity scenes and at Christmas, we remember the shepherds and the wise men who came bearing gifts for a king. What they found instead was an ordinary family, but in temporary accommodation, struggling with a new baby. It must have been quite a shock. The wise men had tried Herod's palace first, but found they got the wrong address. Yet the Gospels record that they still gave their gifts, expensive as they were, and left them at the poor and lowly stable. In their own way, they were quite radical, and they throw a question back to us. What gifts will we give to the homeless, the displaced, the poor and the marginalized? Our response to Jesus must indeed 'cost not less than everything'.

Living

It is not perhaps surprising that we forget – all too easily – that many of the early Christians found themselves, quite quickly, homeless. For being a Bad Jew and a convert to a new religion or sect came at a price. You could lose your parents, children, friends and the roof over your head. Likewise, for the purposes of worship and meeting together, the first Christians were Jews, but aberrant ones who were soon evicted from the synagogues and temple. As such, they were no longer forging their identity through being the children of Abraham or Moses, as their numbers now included Greeks, Romans, Ethiopians; people of different ethnicity, for whom a knowledge of Judaism – let alone any attraction to it – was minimal. Questions, then, of what bound the church together, and to their neighbours, were existential for the early church.

So, the early church, following the mandate of the Kingdom of God as set out by Jesus, was multi-ethnic and anti-tribal. Time and again, writers in the New Testament set out a vision for the church that is parochially focused and engaged and yet universally welcoming. It welcomes the slave and free, male and female, Jew and Greek, old and young, citizen and foreigner. It was not just a mould-breaking faith, but also a caste-crushing religion. In Christ all were equal, just as they were in the eyes and heart of God: equally loved, equally saved, equally cherished and equally bound. This is why attention to what the Covid-19 pandemic has revealed is so important for us now. Namely, the stark divisions still operating within many communities, regions and nations, where the rates of spread, infection and death have highlighted levels of social and economic differentiation – or rather, deprivation. The virus has been harsher on those already struggling with the heat of oppression, hardship, poverty and sickness. The virus does discriminate (Wilkerson, 2020).

The early church, in contrast, was shaped around the indiscriminate love of God. It was a community that cared for all, as Christ had done. Difference did not matter, because to God, each and every one is cherished, and made in the image of God. The diversity of the early church is much like our own today. The promise of Jesus is that we are not left orphaned, or desolate (John 14.15–21). The love of Christ is adoptive in character – we are taken into God's family: we are not born into it. God has many children, but no grandchildren; adoption is not passed on through the family line, but rather renewed in every age with every person.

One of my favourite films is *The Railway Children*. It is a movie for all ages and has enjoyed enduring popularity. The film is closely based on the Edith Nesbit's story, originally serialized in *The London Magazine* during 1905 and first published in book form in 1906. I remember going to see the film at the Crosby Odeon with my grannie in 1970, when it was first released. The film and book concern a family who move out from London to a house in the shires near a railway. Their move was forced upon them, after the father – an intelligent, high-ranking civil servant – was unjustly imprisoned for espionage, but is eventually exonerated.

In their new environs, the three children – Bobbie, Peter and Phyllis – befriend an older gentleman who normally takes the morning train from near their home. He becomes an unlikely hero, for in his empathy for the children, is moved to help prove their father's innocence, thereby reuniting the family. Before the father is freed, however, the family care for a Russian exile who came to England looking for his lost family. And the family also take in and care for Jim, the grandson of the old gentleman.

For a good part of the film, the children are effectively orphaned. The climax is achingly beautiful. The train pulls in and stops, and Bobbie, alone, stands on the platform and waits, not knowing if her father is there. The entire scene is consumed in the steam and smoke of the locomotive. And out of the clouds, the father emerges. As the Gospel says: 'I will not leave you orphaned; I am coming to you' (John 14.18). When we think of orphans, we instinctively think of children without parents. In fact, the English word 'orphan' comes from the Greek *orphanos*, meaning 'bereaved', 'bereft' or 'deprived'. In English, it has come to signify a child losing one or both parents. Of course, we are always somebody's child. Unless we predecease our parents, we will all know what it is to be orphaned: to be without our father or mother. We can be an orphan at any age.

This pandemic has so far led to tens of thousands of deaths in our land, and that number will continue to climb. That means there are hundreds of thousands of new orphans today; and a great many more families, friends and colleagues are also sadly bereft. We only understand the gift of who we truly loved when we experience their loss. At Eastertide, we wait and pause for another loss, even after the crucifixion. For after the resurrection of Jesus comes the ascension. He leaves and returns to the Father. The disciples will be bereft once more – orphaned. Yet the Scriptures promise us an end more like *The Railway Children.*

In the Gospels Jesus refers to the Holy Spirit as 'the Comforter', and it is this name that most closely associates the maternal and paternal comforting care that Jesus gives – so abundantly in his ministry – with what is to come after he has gone. Don't be afraid of the storm, or of sinking in this boat. Do not worry about lack of food or clothes. Do not worry about those who hate you. Do not worry about death. 'Do not be afraid ... I am with you,' says Jesus.

As a child, I grew up always knowing I had been adopted. It has had, and continues to have, a profound influence on my personhood, ministry and theology. Deeply imprinted in my soul is the knowledge that, though I was bereft as a baby, I was not in fact abandoned. I was blessed with good and loving parents, who came for me, and took me home. Interestingly, another meaning of the word 'orphan' is quite general – 'to change allegiance; passing from one status to another'.

That was my experience. My status moved from being an 'unwanted baby' to becoming a much-cherished, much-wanted, much-loved ... son. Many years later, as an adult, my parents told me that I had never in fact been 'un-wanted'. My birth mother simply could not keep me. But she had held me for the first weeks of my life, and only gave me up when she handed me over, in person, to the couple that came for me – my parents. My 'new normal' was to learn that I had always been held and cherished.

The first Christians held, cared for and cherished orphans. The Scriptures give many examples of infants being adopted and raised by folk that are not their biological parents. The early church was called to be an adopting, caring and comforting community for everyone – especially the neglected, marginalized and bereft. The words Jesus speaks to us are what he calls us to proclaim and practice to the rest of humanity today: 'we will not leave you orphaned or bereft; we are here for you; we are coming to you; do not be afraid; God never leaves any of us'. God is love.

Loving

One of my former tutors often used to ask the groups of clergy he was teaching what they thought might be the biggest problem facing the churches today. Without fail, clergy would opine that it was financial or reputational, or perhaps consumerism, individualism and secularization. He would listen with care, but then suggest the biggest problem facing the churches today had never, ever changed. It was, in his words, 'Coping with the overwhelming abundance of God.' It was a striking and disarming statement. Yet it captures something the church often neglects and forget. Paul, in one his letters puts it like this:

> But when the goodness and loving-kindness of God our Saviour appeared, he saved us, not because of any works of righteousness that we had done, but according to his mercy, through the water of rebirth and renewal by the Holy Spirit. This Spirit he poured out on us richly through Jesus Christ our Saviour, so that, having been justified by his grace, we might become heirs according to the hope of eternal life. (Titus 3.4–7)

Note that the kindness and love come to us – unmerited and uninvited. Paul says we can't save ourselves. And yes, Paul's letter to Titus goes on to extol the importance of virtues and good behaviour. But Paul does not add 'or else you'll be for it!' No threats are made. Salvation is not something you eventually acquire after hard work, and only provided you are very, very good. We have all sinned. We all fall short of the glory of God. No one *deserves* heaven. Yet God loves us, fully and completely, as Jesus shows us. I have always thought this was the gospel all good evangelicals proclaimed? Actually, I thought that was the gospel. Full stop.

The Gospels often chide the church for trying to act as a kind of Border Agency Police for heaven; or Christians offering their well-meaning services to Jesus as Immigration Control Officers for paradise. But Jesus isn't interested in our proposals to police the boundaries of his kingdom, thank you. So, the Gospels offer extreme cases of God saying, 'let it be' or 'mind your own business'. The dying thief on the cross is an obvious example (Luke 23.32–43). He could not have known Jesus for more than a few minutes, or perhaps even seconds, let alone an hour.

Yet on the cross, for the most minimal confession, he is promised paradise. Had the disciples still been around to witness this exchange shortly before the death of Jesus they might have wondered to themselves what on earth the point of giving up everything and forsaking all for the Kingdom of God had been. Had they not been with Jesus for three years? Had they not abandoned their jobs? Had they not left behind their families, even leaving the dead unburied? So how is it that Jesus is offering precisely the same – no more and no less to a man who has been committed to a life violence and crime? It doesn't seem fair.

Fairness is something Jesus often asks us to reflect on. The younger son in the parable of the prodigal (Luke 15.11–32) isn't treated fairly at all. He is treated with lavish generosity, and absurd, abundant, unmerited love. The parable of the labourers in the vineyard (Matt. 20.1–16) gives an equal portion of the rewards to the least deserving. God gives those who are apparently quite hopeless the same – the same – as those who have toiled all day long. So many parables and miracles from Jesus remind Christians that God's love and salvation isn't measured out in fractions. You can't be half-saved or half-healed. You can't be half-baptized. You can't be half-loved by God. The love is not conditional: there is no small print or 'terms and conditions apply' caveat. God's love for us is a case of comprehensive assurance. There is a remarkable absence of any 'no-claims-bonus' scheme.

Church congregations have not yet resorted to 'Reward Cards' – extra grace or more time in heaven, the more time you spend in church, and the more you do for God. We are too easily seduced by Ecclesiastical Loyalty Schemes. But, you can't earn God's love. So many of the parables Jesus tells get right under the skin of the real motivation for being part of the church, and following Jesus. And the interesting thing that the parables suggest is that in Christ's scheme of salvation, the rewards and bonuses scheme is rather 'flat'.

The God of surprises that we follow turns out to have a few weaknesses you might not know about, and which have not been the subject for sermons. For one thing, God's heart is too soft – for God is recklessly forgiving. God is colour-blind too. God also seems to lack discernment, often choosing the worst, lowliest and basest things to work with. Love, kindness and kenosis are purposefully hard-wired into what God does in Christ. Our problem is that we are 'closet Pelagians' – deep down, we subscribe to the ancient heresy that believes there is actually quite a lot we can do to can earn our salvation. So, we get busy, hoping Jesus will, after all, reward us. Margery Kempe (1373–1438), an English mystic, had a revelation from God about precisely this, and heard God say to her: 'More pleasing to me than all your prayers, works and penances is that you would believe I love you.' The trouble is, we do – but we keep attaching conditions to God's love – ones that God just deletes from every contract of religion we try to make with the world. It can be maddening, I guess, to discover that God will save whom God wants to save. For this reason, I admire Harry Smart's poem, 'Praise':

Praise be to God who pities wankers
and has mercy on miserable bastards.
Praise be to God who pours his blessing
on reactionary warheads and racists.

For he knows what he is doing; the healthy
have no need of a doctor, the sinless
have no need of forgiveness. But, you say,
They do not deserve it. That is the point;

That is the point. When you try to wade
across the estuary at low tide, but misjudge
the distance, the currents, the soft ground
and are caught by the flood in deep schtuck,

then perhaps you will realize that God
is to be praised for delivering dickheads
from troubles they have made for themselves.
Praise be to God, who forgives sinners.

Let him who is without sin throw the first
headline. Let him who is without sin

build the gallows, prepare the noose,
say farewell to the convict with a kiss.
(Smart, 1995)

Dwelling on the love of God – the absurd, unfair, boundless,
overwhelming love of God poured out in Jesus Christ – can
be almost unbearable. One of my predecessors as Principal of
Cuddesdon was in the habit of running a 'God on Monday
Club' at lunchtime. Ordinands were invited into his study
to talk about God. The only rule was you were not allowed
to talk about anything else. You could not discuss church
politics, or snobbishly pontificate on fashions and practices
in liturgy, preaching and ecclesiastical vestments. You could
not talk about yourself, nor were you permitted to show off
your knowledge on obscure points of doctrine or church history. No, the rule was simple: you could only talk about God.
An hour was set aside for this activity. As my predecessor
remarked many years later, most of these hours passed in sublime, simple silence.

My hunch is that the hour was always doing more than
could be known. To pray is to empty oneself in order to be
filled with the presence of God. That work of self-emptying is
immense, and lifelong. It involves deep attention to our interi-
ority to notice and address the obstacles and clutter that fill the
space, and prevent God from dwelling within us. Sometimes,
we have to forget religion in order to remember God.

Concluding with Likeness

I was recently struck by a survey conducted by a Diocese in
the Church of England. Each person on the Electoral Roll of a
parish was being encouraged to develop their own individual
Personal Discipleship Plan. Everyone was 'to be encouraged to
take personal responsibility for their relationship with God'.
While one could ask profound and searching questions of the
previous two sentences, as with so many of these resource-
based initiatives (yes, the Diocese had things to offer that the

unsuspecting Christian might not ever know they ever needed or wanted), respondents were invited to fill in a questionnaire. One question was, 'Have you ever had a conversation with your vicar that was spiritual or about God, but did not involve you at the same being asked to take on a role or responsibility in your church?' At the time of writing, the response so far from the laity – a full 100 per cent – was 'no'.

The problem, as we have seen, lies in placing the church before the Kingdom of God, and giving the anxieties, pride and status of the church more attention than the person of Jesus. Being like Christ and being Christ-like matters more than anything. Mahatma Gandhi said: 'I like your Christ. I do not like your Christians. Your Christians are so unlike your Christ.' The question is not 'what does the church look like today?' but rather, 'who does the church remind you of?' There is obviously one answer to that question, and it hardly needs stating. A letter published in *The Times* on 27 May 2014 makes the point in a different way:

> Sir, Enoch Powell once attended a country fête and was amused to see an 'Enoch Powell lookalike' competition. On the spur of the moment (and having a much greater sense of humour than he was usually credited with) he entered, incognito. He came third. (John Hurdley – Highclere, Hants)

Christians will always hope to look like Jesus. Indeed, we are called to become like Jesus; to re-semble in our lives the one who is in the image of God. As Paul writes in 2 Corinthians 3.18, 'all of us, with unveiled faces, seeing the glory of the Lord as though reflected in a mirror, are being transformed into the same image from one degree of glory to another; for this comes from the Lord, the Spirit'. But to re-semble means to un-semble.

H. G. Wells once said, 'I am not a believer, but I have to admit, as a historian, that this penniless preacher from Galilee is irrevocably the centre of history.' In Jesus, we find the full grace of God, in all its softness and vulnerability, and yet rooted in and wrapped around the unshakable and undiminished love of God, that yields to no darkness. Jesus is fully 'homed' in divinity and humanity, relishing companionship, but always with the eye and heart to pick up the broken and loving deeply those who have fallen foul of the system. As Desmond Tutu said, 'God has a soft spot for sinners ... God has set a low bar for his love, and for heaven.' I sometimes wonder if the church even has a clue concerning how radical, unconditional and extravagant God's love is?

How then shall we live? St Augustine had a remarkable insight after his conversion: that it was only the merciful humility of God that can penetrate our armoured pride. The church has drunk deep from the proverbial Kool-Aid (an American term for blind adherence to a bad idea), and has followed Dale Carnegie's *How to Win Friends and Influence People* (a bestselling self-help book first published in 1936). But the Gospels and the lives of the saints are only interested in doing the right thing by all people, and are not especially concerned with winning friends, fame or fortune. The gospel calls us to a life of self-sacrifice, not self-fulfilment (Wells, 2019; Williams, 2018b).

Our lives are to be marked by humility, gratitude, gentleness, kindness, faithfulness and solidarity. Our love is to be orientated towards blessing God and our neighbour; and yes, our enemies too. We are called to be the person who God made us to become. In this, we are never fully converted, as our conversion to Christ is always work-in-progress. But in all this, no matter what our struggles, love is our calling. There will be so many reasons to withhold that love, ration it, or make it conditional.[15] But in the end, it is what God has shown us in Jesus, and it is what makes us become more fully human, and more – and more – like the one we are called to re-semble ourselves as. This is a tall order, I know. But fear not. God is patient and kind, and as Paul reminds us, 'when the goodness and loving-kindness of God our Saviour appeared, he saved us, not because of any works of righteousness that we had done, but according to his mercy ....' (Titus 3.4–5). Thanks be to God.

Coda: The Stature of Liberty

Not everything that is faced can be changed,
but nothing can be changed until it is faced.
James Baldwin

This coda intentionally begins with a quote from James Baldwin (1924–87) who was one of the great moral essayists that America produced in the twentieth century. Baldwin was an American novelist, playwright, poet and activist in the Civil Rights movement. He lived much of his adult life in the south of France, where he befriended Miles Davis, Nina Simone and Ray Charles, among others, when they came to play at jazz festivals in Nice. This might seem to us now like quite an array of friends, but we forget that in an era of McCarthyism, the Civil Rights movement and apartheid, the colour of your skin determined where you could eat, and which hotels would take your custom, while others would refuse it. Adding the fear of liberation, equality in sexuality and gender, socialism and communism into the mix, and we find figures such as Dalton Trumbo, who wrote the screenplays for *Spartacus* and *Exodus* (spot the connection), imprisoned in 1950 for 11 months in the federal penitentiary in Ashland, Kentucky for his 'un-American' political leanings. In the Land of the Free and the Home of the Brave, you could be imprisoned for being a communist.

Many of Baldwin's writings explore the prejudices he faced as a gay and black man, growing up in an America that was still segregated, and where all discussion of sexuality was normatively about masculinity. Baldwin's essays (for example, in *Notes of a Native Son*, 1955) delve into the ambiguities and intricacies that he encountered through racial, sexual and class divisions. Steeped in the King James Bible he had learned through his membership of a Baptist church in Harlem, Baldwin's writings literally sweat out the heat of oppression that he grew up with. Themes of humanity and humility jostle with justice, freedom and liberation.

This book has been concerned with humility – personal and ecclesial – and has therefore touched on arenas where the church often presumes to neglect or reject what the world can say to it, and instead, only speaks. This is the church of monologue, not dialogue; a church stuck in broadcast mode, incapable of reception. Frequently, the church behaves as though it possesses the truth, and the world does not. Yet in truth, the church is meant to be possessed by the truth. When this realization takes root, the church humbles itself, finally surrendering our pride-filled fantasy that we are capable of being self-sufficient.

But we are offered a different path, rooted in the example of Jesus, who in his own kenosis, became an exemplar of divine wisdom. In our calling, like Jesus, to become the Verb of God, we cannot do this alone, or in our strength. Through his flesh, his sensate incarnation, preaching and practices, the body of Christ both communicates and receives love. Jesus is like this, and lives like this, because the pattern that God seeks to restore in Christ is relational – one of friendship, in which grace, love and mercy are abundant. Jesus can, in his incarnation, be party to mutual relationships. This is evident in his encounters with Gentiles, where he is willing to listen, learn and to change.

Feasting with God lies at the heart of this. The banquet of the Kingdom of God is a mutual affair with common fare. The equality and capacious, gracious inclusion it models is the only template the church has. Many years ago, a professor of psychology at the University of Louvain took an interest in how people feasted and celebrated (Debuyst, 1968, p. 10). As part of his research, he asked one of his students to write a thesis on the following subject: 'How do children, aged 9–11 years, experience the phenomenon of *feast*?' The student approached the subject in a number of ways, and one of these consisted of showing a controlled group of 100 children three drawings of a different birthday feast.

In the first drawing, the picture depicted a child alone, but before a mountain of gifts and presents waiting to be opened. In the second drawing, the child was not alone, and was surrounded by just a few members of their family, and some food – a birthday cake, ice-cream and other treats. But there were many fewer presents to open – in fact only one parcel, and not very big at that. In the third picture, the child was surrounded by wider family, friends and neighbours, and there was more food. But there was no gift or parcel in the picture at all, so nothing to open. The question the children were asked was simple enough: which of these birthdays would you rather have for yourself, and why?

Seventy per cent of the sample chose the third picture. And they explained, as children might, that this was the real feast. Others said, 'Because in the third picture, everyone is happy – in the first picture, only I am happy, and in the second picture, not enough people are happy.' The children, in other words, grasped something authentic about humanity and sociality. That by being together, and only by being together, can we be truly happy. True, this takes organization, and can be headache for the organizers. But a feast, to be a feast, needs people. A feast is not about 'what's in it for me' or being self-fulfilled. It is about others, as much as ourselves.

A true feast, in Christian terminology, is a communion with God, *and* a communion with people – the two are indivisible. We cannot share at the common table and only be self-interested, any more than we can share in a common feast of the word, and be only there for ourselves. When God bids us welcome – to the feast that George Herbert speaks of in his poem 'Love Bade Me Welcome' – we are invited into a meal and an experience that is collective in character, because God's love is shared. God's feasts are gracious in character; sublime in their fullness, greatness and capacious vision. They draw us in; and they send us out. They are profoundly communal.

One of the deeper currents that stirs within humility is the pull towards equality, mutuality and community – a freedom and liberation that is not at the expense of our neighbours or enemies, but rather something that gathers us up into a richer vein of humanity. As such, humility – the call to be humble – has a serious civic, moral and spiritual dimension that is supposed to have social and political impact. Humility is not possible without truthfulness, and as George Orwell remarked, 'The further a society drifts from truth, the more it will hate those who speak it.' This has become true in our churches too. When truth speaks to power – on areas of gender-justice, sexuality, equality, domestic, spiritual and sexual abuse – the church forgets its humility, and puts on the armour of pride and denial. Reputation is cited as the reason for this, yet the more the church lacks humility and truth, the more the armour rusts and corrodes from the inside.

The Statue of Liberty in New York with its iconic figure of liberty holding aloft the flame of freedom, enlightening the world, is also a beacon of welcome and hope to the immigrants that have, for centuries, poured into America because of religious and political persecution in Europe, or because of economic hardship and famine. At its base is a bronze plaque mounted on the lower level of the statue's pedestal, with a sonnet by the American poet Emma Lazarus (1849–87). The poem is called 'The New Colossus', and Lazarus wrote her poem in 1883 to raise money for the construction of that pedestal:

'Keep, ancient lands, your storied pomp!' cries she
With silent lips. 'Give me your tired, your poor,
Your huddled masses yearning to breathe free,
The wretched refuse of your teeming shore.
Send these, the homeless, tempest-tost to me,
I lift my lamp beside the golden door!'
(Lehman, 2006)

This is a call to the core of America's soul: a place of welcome for all, because together, we find enrichment. But it could just as easily be some Beatitudes for the church in the twenty-first century. In giving, we gain; in receiving, we are renewed and replenished, not diminished. So the church needs to listen to and receive from the voices and lives – spoken truths to power – that come from individuals and groups committed to gender justice; from those marginalized and stigmatized because of their sexuality; those silenced and shunned because of the shame of the church through the abuse it has permitted individuals to suffer and endure, but cannot face or bear to engage with; from current and future generations of younger people, who now no longer trust the church, or believe it to be good and true. We need to listen – and learn. Without humility, the church will be lost to its own self-regard.

True humility promotes justice and truth. True humility listens and learns. True humility turns away from hubris. True humility dares to hope, because it risks dependency on others. So, hope is not simply a virtue, or merely a matter of practice in our personal piety. Hope is a political act. As Angela Davis said, 'We have to act as if it were possible to radically transform the world ... and we have to do this all the time' (Davis, 2011, p. 4). The architecture of hospitality, welcome and reception that shapes the actual Statue of Liberty is rooted in the stature of liberty. It understands that migrants come bearing gifts that enrich the society that is open and kind enough to receive them; that very act of welcome, rooted in humility, leads to a richer humanity.

The late twentieth-century revivalist, John Wimber, was a deft preacher with an easy style of communication. He defined Christianity as 'doin' the stuff', and in many respects, he was right. I recall him once chiding a conference for the seemingly endless parade of bathetic 'prophetic words' which kept hogging the limelight and interrupting the worship, and were only memorable for being so forgettable. He said, 'OK, enough of this. I have a prophecy for the church. Two words: "Wake Up!"' Quite so. Wimber – controversially for his time – took the view that people who were persuaded into Christianity by reasoned arguments were always at the mercy of better ones. While we can also agree that his preference for persuasion by 'signs and wonders' was open to the same problem – at the mercy of more impressive signs and wonders – an underlying truth remains. Namely, churches *doing* things is usually much better than churches saying things.

On this, I could not agree more. Yet our current ecclesial

culture thinks that if we could only just 'do' church better (whether 'messy', 'fresh', 'traditional' or 'alternative', etc.), many more would flood through the doors. I have a retort: 'Don't Do Church – Do God!' To contradict the words of Alastair Campbell (when prime minister Tony Blair was asked in an interview about his Christian faith), 'I'm sorry, we don't do God' (*Daily Telegraph*, 5 May 2003), Christians *are* actually meant to 'do God'. That is the point of *being* a Christian.

Our problem is we think that by attending to the abstract – the church in this case – we fix the problem. So better management and professionalization is often proffered, ushering in more ecclesiocracy. Others prefer to pay attention to techniques for numerical church growth, and place faith in the 'science' of ecclesionomics. Others still, say that we can't fix the church any more, so better to try something entirely new like a boutique gathering that targets niche markets, and so, leave 'inherited' church for some vague gestating 'shape' – but this is a form of ecclesianarchy. None of these solutions deal with the fundamental problem: us. We need to 'do God'; be like Jesus (Williams, 2020).

This means being real and honest about our issues with pride and status, and what it is currently costing the church, and indeed the entire enterprise of furthering the Kingdom of God. If we fear our loss of power and status, we will fall into modes of self-protection that are mainly invested in avoiding humiliation. The striking relationships between humiliation and humility are highlighted across the Gospels. Jesus snubs invitations from the well-to-do in favour of the lowly. Jesus consorts with those who, in the eyes of others, should be well beneath him. In so doing, it becomes apparent that some witnesses find Jesus' humility a source of personal humiliation, as it interrogates their status and self-perception.

In parables too, we find explicit connections between humility and humiliation. For example, a prodigal father sets aside his honour, pride and status (so, self-humiliation) to embrace a lost son, in Luke 15. The older son finds the humiliation of his father too much to bear, and it in turn implies a humiliation of him. In the parable of the debtors (Matt. 18.21–35), the slave who owes everything throws himself at the mercy of his master, to whom he owes everything. It is an act of humiliation and pleading. Jesus says the master has pity, and forgives the debt. To be clear, this is a humble act on the part of the master. However, the slave does not reciprocate, and so proceeds to humiliate those who are his debtors. Instead of passing on the expurgation of his debt, that slave is punitive to those who owe him money, and he punishes them. The parable closes with the master withdrawing forgiveness and mercy from the debt-owing slave, until he has paid in full, thereby humiliating the slave.

In saying 'do God', it is crucial not to underestimate the cost of discipleship. Christianity can easily collapse into niceness and politeness, with true charity being substituted for mere civility. Too often, Christians are happy to be witnesses, but not activists. We watch and comment as bystanders, but we do not get involved. Afraid of getting involved or taking sides, inaction is exactly what permits – in the memorable phrase of Hannah Arendt – the banality of evil to flourish. Churches develop, all too easily, a kind of institutional muteness, selective blindness and partial deafness. Jesus was different and in his ministry keenly sensate towards pain and injustice, as well as apathy and indifference. We are called to be the body of Christ. Courage and wisdom to act is what is needed. Nobody has to wait for the call or a vocation to be discerned. This is what being a Christian means: doing God.

David Morgan (1937–2020) was a sociologist whose first study was on the educational background of Church of England bishops (60 years ago when he wrote his doctorate, most were public school and Oxbridge), and whose last book was a study of snobbery. That subject – snobbery – might seem an unusual note to begin our conclusion. However, we have already seen that class – social spheres, strata, wealth, poverty and opportunity – still determine people's lives in the twenty-first century. As Morgan points out, the ground of our snobbery has shifted in modernity from one of social position to material or cultural possession. We see this at work in religion – high and low church can be snobbish about the other, as can liberals and conservatives. Even religious faith will develop its own 'spiritual snobscape', which can disavow others, or its own inverted snobbery (pride) as a lack of conspicuous consumption, power and possession.

Snobbery derives from complex micro-cultures, which are often rooted in class, but it can also be seen in ethnicity, gender and sexuality. Snobbery – when practised – is permission for one group to gossip about, patronize and perhaps denigrate another group. In recent times, we have seen this in politics (for example, in America and the Brexit debates), economics (certain retail stores and what they are deemed to represent, or fashions and fads), and society (class, career, possessions, aspirations, etc).

It is perhaps a surprise to discover Jesus dealing with spiritual snobbery in quite blunt terms. For example, he tells a story about a Pharisee and a tax-collector (Luke 18.9–14), in which the Pharisee is caricatured as a spiritual snob: 'God, I thank you that I am not like other people – thieves, rogues, adulterers, or even like this tax collector. I fast twice a week: I give a tenth of all my income.' In contrast, the tax-collector stands at a distance from the altar, and prays humbly. Jesus concludes, 'for all who exalt themselves will be humbled, but all who humble themselves will be exalted'.

Philip North, the Bishop of Burnley has repeatedly warned the Church of England that it has often failed to understand how middle-class, white and comfortable it has become.[16] A kind of ecclesial narcolepsy has developed, with dioceses and congregations failing to recognize their visible and invisible classist assumptions. This is strange when one considers how chapel and church distinctions in the recent past often pivoted on class as much as belief. Or, for that matter, how early Pentecostal churches and their distinctiveness were earthed in class and ethnicity, not just on emphases on religious experience. Indeed, H. R. Niebuhr's *The Social Sources of Denominationalism* was keenly aware of how elite Episcopalians were, in contrast, say, to poorer inner-city congregations. Niebuhr addressed the ethical failure of the divided church as a whole, and the very existence of what he termed 'churches of the disinherited'. He named the churches of the middle-class, and critiqued the nationalism, sectionalism and denominationalism in America. He wrote compellingly of the churches of the immigrants, the colour lines that divide cities and churches, and called for repentance and a commitment to integrated unity.[17]

In the twenty-first century, we need to become far more conscious of the emerging dividing lines that are separating society and splitting communities. New alloys of belief can be beguiling. For example, left-wing individualism (which can be doctrine in almost any mainstream political party in the developed world) presumes that what all people need is opportunity, a level playing field, education and graft. True, equality should give everyone an equal chance. And this makes it easier for us to place our faith in, as the philosopher Michael Sandel notes, 'the rhetoric of rising', which lauds those who achieve well, precisely because we assume everyone deserves the level they attain (Sandel, 2020).

Deep down, however, we know that this fabled 'level playing field' is a chimera. It is an ideal, not an actuality. There will always be exceptions to the rule; but the rule is what persists. Meritocracy is a fine and noble ideal. But it is a dangerous delusion if we presume that, as all are born equal, equality is easily retained. For in the business of how we are raised and developed, some are more equal than others, and will therefore go on to achieve different results. In this, we would do well to remember that the early churches did not impose parity on its members or neighbouring churches based on merit or results. Rather, the parity proposed by the Kingdom of God lay in the equality of human condition and value embodied in Jesus' ministry. It was by treating everyone as equal, that the crippled, stigmatized, diseased and demonized regained their full citizenship. They could now hold their heads high, as they became participants in a common venture. The early church did not preach equality of opportunity: it preached equality of value.

It will seem oxymoronic to some that any Dean of Christ Church writes any sort of book about humility and humiliation. Yet in the course of thinking through this book, I have been continually struck by the deep connections between humility and reciprocity, and the authentic, grounded life to which we are called. More personally, I have found myself accompanied by and cared for individuals and groups severely damaged in their lives by the church. Many of these people have suffered sexual abuse from clergy and church leaders, which has been covered up for years. Others have been falsely accused, and treated as though guilty. They have much in common, for in their cries to be heard by the church – listened to and cared for – they have been denied truth and justice, and instead marginalized and stigmatized. One might have thought that people brought this low – reduced to rubble and ruin, often – would have nothing left but their anger. But it is not so. In their enduring humanity, they have behaved with integrity, modelled fortitude and tenacious morality, and have shown no sign of relinquishing their courage, compassion and concern to put the wrongs right. In my friendships and work with them, I have often been reminded of Anna Akhmatova's poem 'If All Who have Begged Help':

If all who have begged help
From me in this world,
All the holy innocents,
Broken wives, and cripples,
The imprisoned, the suicidal –
If they had sent me one kopeck
I should have become 'richer
Than all Egypt ...'
But they did not send me kopecks,
Instead they shared with me their strength,
And so nothing in the world
Is stronger than I,
And I can bear anything, even this.
(Akhmatova, 2006, p. 173)

There is an inherent political aspect to true humility, since at its most supine, it can be read as something like the Machiavellian inaction of Uriah Heep in Charles Dickens' *David*

Copperfield (1850), a character notable for his cloying humility, unctuousness, obsequiousness and insincerity, who is often found making frequent references to his own 'umbleness'. It is perhaps strange then, to realize that humility is not only about surrender, but also about resistance – and this resistance requires real resolve and strength. Humility is not capitulation to anything and everything. Rather, as Melinda McGarrah Sharp puts it,

> resistance is oppositional, it involves using human agency for change to oppose something ... [it is] courageous, righteous, prophetic, social, visionary, just, creative, and more. (McGarrah Sharp, 2020, p. 4)

McGarrah Sharp goes on to explain the reasons that many invest in not seeking change. Perhaps this is 'not me', or I am 'not there', and so cannot help. Perhaps the time is 'not now', and the ideas for change 'not relevant' or 'not possible'. These stances are so easy to adopt, even in the most switched-on churches, but they are rooted in the pride that refuses to stoop, and get involved – to be genuinely incarnate and engaged in the struggles of others for justice, which is inherently messy, ambiguous and uncertain. Why, after all, would anyone 'interfere' in a situation where we are unsure that we detect abuse or injustice, whether this be domestic, sexual, or other forms?

Yes, we could be wrong. It is always easier to do nothing and keep silent. But as Judith Herman reminds us in her classic *Trauma and Recovery*, 'all the perpetrator asks is that the bystander does nothing' (Herman, 1992, p. 7). If we keep on doing nothing, we will learn nothing new; and so, we will believe nothing that contradicts what we thought was already true, or unchangeable. Humility, then, accepts that by facing up to our not knowing, we might have to act *now*. Humility means Jesus *does* things: washes feet; speaks to people others would not have the time of day for; questions injustice when for all the bystanders, there was seemingly nothing wrong to even query. The enticement we all face is clear. In failing to question and to then act, we will maintain some pride and dignity (for what this is worth), but our lack of humility actually permits a worse state of affairs. The only thing necessary for the triumph of evil is that good people do nothing.

To be sure, our present age is not for the faint-hearted. Our churches, for the most part, remain remarkably resilient communities of grace in these demanding times. Some days, it is not easy to plan for tomorrow, never mind outline a strategy or vision that might inspire us (and even work?) for the next ten years. Too often, such talk in the recent past has turned out to be mere chimera. We need new purpose and direction, not based on survival, but service; not rooted in preserving social status, but in spiritual wisdom to enrich the world. It is tempting to anticipate the future, and many leaders try and 'get ahead of the curve' (or use other clichés that infer they can see around the corner, or over the horizon). I have met a number of bishops who are setting 'strategic directions' for their diocese, rooted in the latest managerial textbooks, or trendiest of-the-moment treatise on leadership (Tetlock and Gardner, 2016).

I am not convinced this will help the church unless it engages in a more fundamental root-and-branch search for its own soul. The recovery of our humility – grounded in Jesus who humbled himself – is a core calling for Susan Beaumont's remarkable book, *How to Lead When You Don't Know Where You are Going*. The book speaks to our time, and asks how we might lead bodies when the old way of doing things no longer works, but a way forward is not yet clear? Beaumont suggests that these liminal moments in our communal evolution are 'seasonal-threshold times', when the continuity of tradition disintegrates, and uncertainty about the future fuels fears, doubts and disorder. She argues that it is not helpful to pretend we understand what needs to happen next. But leaders can still lead, provided they are humble, can learn from their mistakes, and learn from the present as well as the past.

One of the key tests of our church leadership in the present and the future must rest with restoring the concept of faithfulness and fruitfulness, which are quite different from the concepts of success and results that the world around us may value. If the church tries to mimic the goals and aspirations of the secular organizations that surround it, Christianity will almost certainly have taken a wrong turn:

> Consider your own call, brothers and sisters: not many of you were wise by human standards, not many were power-ful, not many were of noble birth. But God chose what is foolish in the world to shame the wise; God chose what is weak in the world to shame the strong. (1 Cor. 1.26–27)

What is needed now is prophetic action, but also strategic patience; resolve and renewal, but also reflection and reforma-tion. One key root in this is humility, and the development of a humble church that understands its core duties and obliga-tions are first and foremost to God and to society, not to loyal paid-up members of some religious Supporters' Club. Yes, love God with all your heart, mind, soul and strength; and your neighbour as yourself. Yet your neighbour is wholly 'other', as Jesus reminds us: not the familiar and friendly, but rather the one we hoped we might not have to entertain, let alone help us and bless us (Luke 15). The story of a 'good' Samaritan was not one that would have been welcomed by a Judean audi-ence. In telling it, Jesus reminds his listeners to be humble, and understand that God will use any vessel of grace to feed, help, sustain and support us.

Christianity is a faith of conscription, not subscription. We don't elect to donate or contribute in order to receive some-thing back. When you decide to follow Christ, you have been adopted into a new kinship, and you are asked to surrender yourself. You have not bought into a faith that comes with some kind of reward card benefits scheme that offers bonuses for loyal customers. In our time, and for this era, our churches need a serious reset. We have to ask ourselves if we are trying to be member-based organizations, or support-based institutions?

The distinction may not seem obvious at first glance, but the difference can be as night and day. Member-based organ-izations exist to please their members, and their appeal can be quite narrow. In contrast, support-based institutions have members, but they are there to appeal to the public. Political parties often learn the difference the hard way: on polling day. It is one thing to increase political party membership with the right rhetoric and attractive policies. But a larger membership is pointless if your vote halves, and the public desert you. The point of politics, rather like religion, is not to please the membership and ideological loyalists. It is, rather, to be in a position to make changes for the better for everyone. In other words, to be in government. Or, if you prefer, actually beginning to establish the Kingdom of God on earth.

Kenosis will always be for us something of a paradox. Because the love can be fierce; just as the passion is a wilful act of determination, not resignation. Moreover, this love can manifest itself in righteous anger, and even make space for disruptive acts of prophetic leadership. It must make space for peace, joy, hope, patience and kindness too – and so be formed by God's grace. Humility is often a determined act of moral, social and political resistance. In not clinging to status, situations are changed; religion and society are disrupted. The standard ways of living are interrogated. Jesus' humility was often disruptive, and at times, constructively destructive. This intriguing poem from Piers Plowright contrasts Jesus Christ with some of the fickle alternatives:

Considering the other Gods
Would you really want them round your place?
Thor banging about in the hall
Kali destroying the kitchen
Aphrodite coming on strong
In the bedroom – then turning nasty.
All tricksy, changeable – to hell with right and wrong.
I think I'll stick with Jesus:
His half-smile, fierce love,
Amazing Grace.

Mind you, he too could send the plates flying,
Turn things upside down,
The maddened swine stampeding

Into the wine-dark sea,
The wrong pardoned,
And all that crying.

Still he's the one for me
As the world darkens
And drunk captains run the ship.
He's there, in the eye of the storm,
On the cruel tree, facing it down,
Throwing across time and space,
Beyond ambition, pride, the dip of Fate,
A thin line of light
That we can grab before we drown.
(Plowright, 'Choosing', 2019)

The 'drunk captains run the ship' tells us that we often have the wrong leaders in politics and religion. They are often inebriated with their own propaganda, and obsessed with their reputation and legacy. Jesus is not interested. He is humiliated on the cross in the eyes of the world. But in the being of God, this is humility: 'obedient unto death, even death on a cross' (Phil. 2.8). Or, as Plowright has it, 'on the cruel tree, facing it down' turns out be our true lifeline – that 'thin line of light' we can now clutch lest we drown in our own hubris.

But it is costly to go against the grain, and swim against the current. One of my theological heroes is the Irish Dominican Fr Herbert McCabe (1926–2001). I only heard him lecture a couple of times, but it was electrifying. As editor of *New Black-friars*, he called for nuclear disarmament, inveighed against the US involvement in Vietnam, and as a friend of John Hume took a constructive and passionate interest in solving the Northern Ireland Troubles. The Vatican edged him out of the editor-ship of *New Blackfriars* for some years, but he regained the editorial chair in 1970, and predictably picked up his second stint as editor with the words: 'As I was saying before I was so oddly interrupted ...'

McCabe was a radical precisely because of his loyalty to orthodoxy and tradition, not in spite of it. He saw that the tradition we followed was deeply subversive of the prevailing powers and forces at work in our world. His theological writing resounds with pithy aphorisms. 'Jesus died of being human' is one; 'Christ is present in the Eucharist as the meaning is present in a word' is another. And perhaps most tellingly of all for us, he wrote that 'If you don't love, you're dead; and if you do love they'll kill you.'

So at the centre of his faith, and of ours, was this figure of Jesus, who in one sense could be seen as a failed, reviled, humiliated political criminal from Palestine, and whose execution was a grim warning sign of how far the powers of this world are prepared to go when their interests are threatened. For McCabe, as for me, God was and is a matter of weakness rather than power. Jesus' humility is a willed-way-of-being. The subversive power of Jesus comes through the incarnation and the cross. Power made perfect in weakness is what kenosis is ultimately about: humble and obedient 'unto death'. Then, and only then, can there be resurrection. Do not cling to what you think will keep you going. Let go; let God.

In the last days of his life, Helmuth James von Moltke – who had led the German resistance to Hitler – and faced execution at the hands of his Nazi captors, wrote from jail to his wife:

> My life is finished and I can say of myself: he died in the fullness of years and of life's experience. The task for which God made me is done. I end by saying to you by virtue of the treasure that spoke from me and filled this humble earthen vessel: 'The Grace of our Lord Jesus Christ and the love of God and the fellowship of the Holy Spirit be with you all. Amen.' (von Moltke, 1991, p. 85)

I say this because the church sometimes clings to life because it over-imagines the indignity of death. It conflates death with failure and humiliation with humility. So, it keeps on talking (and talking) about life and growth, forgetting that it is God alone who gives these. In one of Dietrich Bonhoeffer's sermons, he writes:

It is not we who are to build, but God. No human being builds the church, but Christ alone. Anyone who proposes to build the church is certainly already on the way to destroying it, because it will turn out to be a temple of idolatry, though the builder does not intend that or know it. We are to confess, while God builds. We are to preach, while God builds. We are to pray to God, while God builds. We do not know God's plan. We cannot see whether God is building up or taking down. It could be that the times that human beings judge to be times for knocking down structures would be, for God, times to do a lot of building, or that the great moments of the church from a human viewpoint are, for God, times for pulling it down.

It is a great comfort that Christ gives to the church: 'You confess, preach, bear witness to me, but I alone will do the building, wherever I am pleased to do so. Don't interfere with my orders. Church, if you do your own part right, then that is enough. But make sure you do it right. Don't look for anyone's opinion; don't ask them what they think. Don't keep calculating; don't look around for support from others. Not only must church remain church, but you, my church, confess, confess, confess' ... Christ alone is your Lord; by his grace alone you live, just as you are. Christ is building. (Bonhoeffer, 2012, pp. 85–6).

Ultimately a humble church is a free church. A church that divests itself of its peripheral concerns and core anxieties, and is rooted in humility and service, and not devoted to its own exaltation, and is prepared even to let go into death, is the same life of kenosis Jesus calls us into. This is the church to be longing for: a down-to-earth body, like Jesus, that abides and dwells richly in the world, to transform it. Scott Cairns has written this poem, taking the Beatitudes (Matt. 5) as his cue. In so doing, he extends the intentionality of Jesus into the terrain we might then find ourselves journeying into, and in the flesh we inhabit as free, humble pilgrims; as a pilgrim people who can through our love and resistance, in our political, pastoral and prophetic living and loving, bring about the radical changes that the Kingdom of God still yearns to usher in:

> Blessed as well are the wounded but nonetheless kind,
> for they shall observe their own mending.
> Blessed are those who shed their every anxious defence,
> for they shall obtain consolation.
> Blessed are those whose sympathy throbs as an ache,
> for they shall see the end of suffering.
> Blessed are those who do not presume,
> for they shall be surprised at every turn.
> Blessed are those who seek the God in secret,
> for they shall hear His very voice rising as a pulse.
> Blessed moreover are those who refuse to judge,
> For they shall forget their most grave transgressions.
> Blessed are those who watch and pray, who seek and plead,
> for they shall see, and shall be heard.
> (Cairns, 'Late Sayings', 2017)

We are all invited to relocate ourselves and our churches within the humility that Jesus embodies. We are called to be the Verb of God too. To practise kindness, and to be authentically humble; and to exceed in love even to those who might seek to humiliate you. We are called to that most tender love – yet fierce and compassionate – for the world in all its brokenness, thirst, hunger and sometimes hatred. So, do not be afraid of what may come. There will be humiliations, naturally. Indeed, it is often in waiting patiently, hoping, trusting and kenosis that we are *refined* – re-sembled and re-formed to become those humble, joyful, kind, patient, courageous, compassionate, prophetic, gentle and faithful people that God calls us all to be.[18]

We live in challenging times. As Evelyn Underhill once remarked, if Christ was small enough to be comprehended, God would not be big enough to worship. Hard though it can be to follow Jesus today, and model our lives on this Verb of God made flesh that we can barely grasp (let alone begin to comprehend) we are bidden time and time again, 'come, follow', and to leave all else behind, all that would prevent and impede us from following. We are called to be Christians, to become Christ-like; and not to settle for being Christ-fans – merely dedicated admirers. Our call now is to See, Judge, Act and Do.

Study Guide for Groups and Individuals

This section contains suggestions and exercises for groups and individuals to aid further reflection. Some are simple and will work as discussion-starters if you are using the text to ruminate on some of the main themes that the book touches on. For convenience these are broken down thematically, although readers will be able to mix, match and adapt these ideas over the course of discussions.

Humble

Personal

- Drawing on the 'Beginnings' illustration based on John 13, invite members of the group to think through and discuss their experiences of humbling themselves. Were these actions conscious and deliberate, or instinctive and responsive?

- How did your becoming humble in a situation change each person?
- When were you last moved and struck by the humility and humble service of someone else, and what form did this take?

Church

- How does your church live out its vocation to be humble in the communities that it serves?
- When do people outside your church experience its pride and hubris, and what can be done to overcome this?
- What can be done to help our churches to focus on 'missional humility'?

Humility

How might the words from these writers below help us reshape our ministries?

- 'Humility is throwing oneself away in complete concentration on something or someone else' (Madeleine L'Engle).
- 'Selflessness is humility. Humility and freedom go hand in hand. Only a humble person can be free' (Jeff Wilson).
- 'Have more humility. Remember you don't know the limits of your own abilities. Successful or not, if you keep pushing beyond yourself, you will enrich your own life – and maybe even please a few strangers' (A. L. Kennedy).

How can we become 'the Verb of God' in our communities and society?

Culture

Much of our modern culture was formed and informed by religious faith and belief. However, much of modern culture now challenges faith anew, pressing questions that have not been asked of churches before. Given this, discuss:

- What can the church learn from the world today, and from what spheres might the world help reform the church for better?
- How can faith challenge our culture anew, not just by providing solutions but also by posing new questions?
- How can faith and culture work together, in a relationship of humility and mutual respect, to enrich contemporary culture?

Salvation

God loves everyone equally. Christ died for all. The idea of salvation is extremely complex. The New Testament offers several different ideas and images of what God accomplishes in Christ. Our concept of salvation will directly influence and shape how we live, evangelize, and interact with the people around us. Given that, discuss the following:

- What does salvation mean for you and your church today?
- Is salvation a matter of what you know and believe personally? Or is salvation something that was done for you, and you do for others?
- When does salvation become realized for you and for others, and is it something you are always aware of?
- Is everyone saved, or is salvation just a gift for a select few?

Owning Our Faith

As churchgoing in the developed world continues to decline, these exercises are designed to help you locate your faith and own it.

- Is your faith the result of a cultural or family tradition – something you were raised with – or because you made a conscious decision?
- Sundays are no longer what they used to be, and for many people are now days off work or time set aside for shopping and recreational activity. When did you become conscious that you spent your Sundays differently to your neighbours, friends and colleagues?
- Deep down, what do you really believe? If following Jesus was and is your decision, what practical differences does this make to your life, and the lives of others?
- 'If being a Christian today were criminal, would there be enough evidence to convict you?' Where and when would this Christian witness be most apparent, and difficult to conceal?

Food for Thought

The Eucharist provides us with a pattern of sharing, equality and humility in the life of Jesus. He takes bread and wine, and invites us to give thanks for God's loving communion with us, and the call to extend that communion between us, and with the wider world. If Jesus is the bread that nourishes us, then:

- In the setting of a traditional Eucharist, we are often given an Old Testament reading, a psalm, a new Testament reading, and a passage from one of the Gospels. So, each Eucharist will have four portions of Scripture. If you are working with this Study Guide in groups over several weeks, ask each person to choose their four portions – the ones that mean the most to them – and how and why this matters to their life.
- What kind of 'spiritual food' is your church offering to the local community? Is it gourmet, home-cooking, fast-food, canteen ... or something else?
- When people think of the spiritual food your church offers to the wider world, is it perhaps far too hard to digest; or maybe just 'not for them'; or perhaps too cheap, and not nutritious enough?

- The first Christian communities were households of faith, and they fed not only their members, but also took care of the widows and orphans. What does it mean for us today to be sharing our food with others?
- When Jesus ate with others, he was often criticized for the company he kept. What do we learn from the Gospels about the Kingdom of God and salvation through feasting and food from the parables and the practices of Jesus?
- Making a humble pie requires ingredients and imagination. Remembering the words of Emma Lazarus:

Give me your tired, your poor,
Your huddled masses yearning to breathe free,
The wretched refuse of your teeming shore.
Send these, the homeless, tempest-tost to me ...

Discuss what your church is doing or could do to gather, welcome and support those on the margins of your community and wider society.

Normativity and Diversity

Churches often evolve over time into associations where people are at ease with one another. While that is quite a natural development for any regular gathering, it can lead to there being 'normal' or 'average' members of a church, and therefore others who are 'different' – either because of class, age, ethnicity or identity.

- Thinking carefully about your own church for a moment, are there 'normative' indications of membership?
- If you can identify some of the normative characteristics of a member of your church, who from the wider community might sense that they were 'different' if they began to attend?
- If your church is set on becoming more diverse, and 'common' in relation to your local culture, what steps are being taken to enable this? What might a commitment to unity and diversity mean for your church?

Jesus

There are over 40 healing miracles in the Gospels. Very rarely do we ever learn the name of the person healed (ten unnamed lepers; the blind and the lame; although we do learn Bartimaeus' name, we never learn the name of Jairus' daughter). Some of the Gospel stories about healing are very short, and some, for example in John's Gospel, much longer. Sometimes the healings are social or moral in character (Zacchaeus, the woman caught in adultery, etc.). In your group, take it in turns to select a story of healing, and apply the questions from the 'Us and Them' chapter:

• Who is this miracle for (poor, tainted, lame, leper, etc.)?
• What does the miracle involve (touch, conversation, etc.)?
• Where and when does it happen (religious building [rare], Gentile or Jewish territory, on the Sabbath, after a long period of affliction, etc.)?
• Why did Jesus heal this person, and in front of these witnesses, and for what ends (because they were marginalized, stigmatized, ostracized, etc.)?
• In view of your discussion, ask the WWJD question of your church, community, or parish: What Would Jesus Do?
• How can our churches become the 'Verb of God' in our communities and in wider society? What would it mean for us as individuals and congregations to 'do God' in our neighbourhood?

God

'Dwelling on the love of God – the absurd, unfair, boundless, overwhelming love of God poured out in Jesus Christ – can be almost unbearable. One of my predecessors as Principal of Cuddesdon was in the habit of running a "God on Monday Club" at lunchtime. Ordinands were invited into his study to talk about God. The only rule was you were not allowed to talk about anything else' (from 'Endings', page 155). As an exercise, try this. Remember, you cannot talk about anything or anyone other than God.

Margery Kempe (1373–1438) said that God revealed these words to her: 'More pleasing to me than all your prayers, works and penances is that you would believe I love you'. Why do you think we struggle to believe this?

'The Gospels often chide the church for trying to act as a kind of Border Agency Police for heaven; or Christians offering their well-meaning services to Jesus as Immigration Control Officers for Paradise. But Jesus isn't interested in our proposals to police the boundaries of his kingdom, thank you' (from 'Endings', p. 152).

- What are the borders and boundaries in your church and denomination?
- Who is policing them? And perhaps more importantly, why?

The Holy Spirit

In the chapter 'Thy Kingdom Come', several examples are given of the Holy Spirit being given the freedom to come to the church through the insights of people who are not part of it. Because the Holy Spirit works inside and outside the church, and is ahead of all our mission, the churches need to become more receptive.

- If we could listen to what the Holy Spirit was saying to the churches from the world, what would we hear?
- If we could hear what the world *thinks* the churches are saying and doing, would we be surprised at how contemporary culture might view our faith and belief today?
- Instead of monologue, dialogue. Instead of only broadcasting, tune in and get some reception. What is the Holy Spirit saying to the churches today?

The Bible

The cultural traditions of the Bible are very different from our social norms today: for example, we don't accept slavery. So how should we apply biblical texts to society today? How should we use the Scriptures to address current issues such as equal marriage, gender roles, immigration reform and other areas? Are there both general principles and specific directives that the Bible gives us?

Other Exercises

- On humility, reflect on and discuss what status you have, and when and if it can be set aside, and to what end.
- What is appropriate for forming the character of a congregation around the humility and self-emptying of Jesus?
- How should churches resist and challenge contemporary culture, and in what spheres should congregations and denominations be taking a stand?
- As an exercise, rewrite the Christ hymn from Philippians 2.5–11 for your church, replacing 'Christ Jesus' with 'our church', 'us' and 'we'. What is our calling in the light of this?

Epilogue: No Sign Shall Be Given, Except the Sign of Jonah

One of the strange details to note in the Gospels is how often Jesus repeats himself. It is not that often, in fact. So when he does, we should pay particular attention, and the 'Sign of Jonah' phrase is uttered twice, in near-identical ways (see Matt. 12.39 and 16.4). Traditionally, the interpretive key to this phrase has been the equation between Jonah's 72 hours in the belly of a whale, and Jesus' two-night, three-day burial after his crucifixion, ending at the resurrection. So, the Pharisees Jesus is talking to in the Gospels – 'this evil and adulterous generation' – are being equated to the citizens of Nineveh. The invitation in both contexts is to repent.

However, we should question such habitual readings of Jesus' words. There are several signs signalled to the reader in the book of Jonah. The perilous storm-tossed sea that nearly drowns all on board the ship to Tarshish, while Jonah sleeps below deck, prefigures the account of Jesus and the disciples in a storm (Mark 4.35–41). The storm is only calmed, and crew and passengers saved, by Jonah's voluntary self-sacrifice. This is a sign.

Later, the prophet is content to take for granted the gift of shade from a bush (Jonah 4.6), but then resents its shrivelling loss. These signs, and others that we encounter in Jonah only point to one conclusion. God is love. God spared Nineveh, including the animals (Jonah 4.1–11), and it made Jonah angry, because Jonah wanted Nineveh punished for their sins, but had suspected all along that God was going to be soft-hearted. God duly delivered, and relented. God forgives. Jonah was extremely miffed with God, and his griping and sulking at God's abundant love and compassion quickly turns to regret and bitterness at even bothering to obey God in the first place. Was pursuing this vocation over land and sea ever worth the bother of leaving home for, Jonah asks himself?

The answer hinges on reading the signs of the times – then, as now. God called Jonah to take the risk of journey, and so play a part in creating the space and time for Nineveh to turn back to God. Jonah duly delivered, but only after he had been made to turn himself over to his fellow-travellers on the ship, into the sea and return to Nineveh. Jonah, in effect, becomes a sign in his own right. God gives us all second chances (and third, fourth and more …), because God is love, and the door of his heart is always open. So there is always hope. Yes, hope: do not despair. But to signal this in signs – then, as now – requires humility and prophetic courage.

One remarkable modern example of a sign of hope in the twenty-first century took place in Ukraine in 2004, when the opposition politician Victor Yushchenko was campaigning for the presidency. He suddenly became gravely ill, and as we now know, he had been poisoned (as a result of which, to this day he remains facially disfigured). Despite this, he was resolved to continue as a candidate. He carried on in hope. Many continued to follow him in hope. On election day, a few weeks after his poisoning, Yushchenko was leading by a significant margin in the votes. Suspicions were therefore raised when the ruling party announced themselves as the victors, briefing the state-owned TV station to run the line: 'Ladies and gentlemen, we announce that the challenger, Victor Yushchenko, has been decisively defeated.'

However, during this live transmission, a translator for the deaf community at the side of the TV screen broadcast, and by the name of Nataliya Dmytruk, was suddenly faced with a stark moral choice. Should she translate what was being read and said, or communicate what everyone really knew? She chose hope, and with considerable courage, Dmytruk refused to translate the scripted words of state TV. Instead, she signed: 'I'm addressing all the deaf citizens of Ukraine … they are lying and I'm ashamed to translate those lies ... Yushchenko is our president.'

Many, many deaf viewers and sign language users were startled by the disruptive contrast in scripted words being said and read by the newsreader, and Dmytruk signing in the corner of the screen. Viewers moved to action by this courageous act of resistance began to contact their friends, families and networks to raise awareness of Dmytruk's message. This in turn moved journalists and the media to investigate and interrogate the events surrounding the election. The Orange Revolution began soon after, when a million people dressed in orange descended on the capital, Kiev, to protest against the fraudulent outcome of the election. Held to account by the people, the ruling party were forced to hold a new election, in which Yushchenko was declared the rightful winner.

As with Kiev, so with Nineveh. To be the Verb of God is to speak and act with prophetic courage and humility, and be vessels of God's love and compassion. So, if we can begin to work out who Jesus Christ is for us today, what does renewing the body of Christ mean for us now and tomorrow? These days there is much talk and much ink spilt in discussing the renewal of the church. But what kinds of renewal are we meant to strive for?

Renewal has many meanings. It could mean resuming something after a lapse or pause (peace talks or conflict). It could mean maintaining continuity (renewing your insurance or membership). It can mean improving something (a building or society). It can mean the retrieval of something that was apparently lost or decimated (a practice or a forest after a devastating fire). It can mean restoration. It can even mean revolution. I take it that our churches will want to enter into all of these possibilities if we wish to face and engage with the challenges we now face in contemporary culture.

The renewal of the body of Christ can only come when we have learned to feel, touch, embrace and heal the pains of the world as Jesus did. To refract an old saying, 'Jesus was not just tough on disease, but also tough on the causes of disease; and not just tough on pain, but tough on the causes of pain.' When he heals a person, Jesus nearly always challenged the social context and culture that framed those disorders and diseases. Jesus hears the dumb; he speaks to the deaf; he sees the blind; and he touches the untouchable. The body of Christ was richly sensate. Jesus discards hubris to embrace humility, and sets aside status for a life and ministry of service. Christianity is not a faith of subscription, but of conscription: we are not paying for some provision. We serve the one who has already paid. To follow Jesus is to waive your rights, not exercise your choices on a take-it-or-leave it basis. Christianity is duty, obligation and joy.

Giving oneself totally to Christ was not meant to be an abstract concept or an enlarged capacity for pious thoughts. Christianity needs to be both concrete and communal. Freedom in Christ is both a gift and a responsibility; it means to live within the truth. The international Young Christian Workers movement – who were very active in the first half of the twentieth century, and later known as Jocists – began with the work of Fr Joseph Cardijn. He attributed the death of his father, a Belgian mineworker, to the harsh conditions that the working-class had to endure. At the time, most working-class Belgians saw the church as serving the interests of the aristocracy. Cardijn devoted his ministry to 'reconciling the Church with industrial workers of the world'. The Young Christian Workers (Jocists) had a motto: 'See, Judge, Act'.

'See' meant to be awake to the realities around us. 'Judge' was a command to soberly discern the meaning of those realities in the light of what we know to be true, especially from the teachings of Christ. 'Act' meant we are required to resist evil: to 'do God'. This is where many of us get stuck, because the difficulty Christians face today is that dialogue and tolerance are the new ecumenism, and they are sometimes put to work to disarm and ultimately defeat unaware ambassadors and exemplars of truth. We must note that conservatives and liberals alike struggle in such a climate. Niceness, tribalism and individualism will always inhibit spoken truth.

To be the Verb of God – to 'do God' – will sometimes not give us the comforts of compromise and reflection. Sometimes dialogue and tolerance will not be right. Truth and justice will be more important. Those who seek to mute faith will always counsel caution and compromise, or pausing and postponement. Yet we need to remember that Christ and Christianity are not about creating happy admirers. We are not here to increase subscribers to Christianity. The admirer and subscriber plays it safe. They may be ecstatic in praising God, and amplify how much they prize *their* faith. They may be inexhaustible in excitable devotion. Yet admirers and subscribers tend not to make sacrifices.

Following Jesus means a whole-hearted, whole-bodied, whole-life surrender. The message of Christianity is simple enough. It is better to die for the truth, than to live for lies. We are called to be God's dissidents: to sit apart, to disagree, to protest about the way the world is. We are also called to act, and to be God's saboteurs. Jesus turning over the tables of the tat-sellers and the money-changers in the temple is a serious sign: plan, dare, do, disrupt. If you are a Christian, you will be a dissenter.

As C. S. Lewis noted in *Mere Christianity*, the world is effectively enemy-occupied territory. For Lewis, Christianity was the saga of the rightful king (Aslan) who has landed, albeit disguised, and is now calling us to take part in his 'great campaign of sabotage'. If we 'do God', we will dissent from the world. Our mission now is to build serious resistances to the occupation of this world, and therefore hold before us the memory and the example of those saints, martyrs, resisters and dissenters, who have gone before us.

This is why Christ's church exists for non-members, just as the Kingdom of God was inaugurated to include the excluded. Tribalism and populism were rejected by Jesus. The body of Christ was founded to be incorporative, and our mission as the church is to constantly renew ourselves in becoming nothing less than a vessel of God's foolish, reckless love, and power made perfect in weakness.

In closing, it is well worth remembering that you will never, ever, in all your life, meet someone that God does not love

– fully, wholly and abundantly – madly and excessively, in fact. Equally, you will never meet anyone who deserves all of this love, or who merits more or less than God's own love for you. You will never meet a person that God does not long to draw into an intense relationship of truth, peace, love, joy and mutual blessing. With this in our mind – and in our actions – that should help the humble church find its place in the world, and understand how best to serve our neighbours and communities. Renewed.

We live in challenging times. Our call is to See, Judge, Act and Do. All faithful Christians before us have done so, and those that come after us will do so likewise. So, as we journey on – actively, humbly, prayerfully and joyfully – let us go in peace to love and serve the Lord.

Bibliography

Aitken, J., 2005, *Porridge and Passion*, London: Continuum.

Akhmatova, A., 2006, *Anna Akhmatova: Poems*, trans. Thomas, D. M., New York: Knopf.

Alizart, Mark, 2020, *Dogs: A Philosophical Guide to Man's Best Friend*, Cambridge: Polity Press.

Allain-Chapman, J., 2018, *The Resilient Disciple: A Lenten Journey from Adversity to Maturity*, London: SPCK.

Alonso, P., 2011, *The Woman Who Changed Jesus: Crossing Boundaries in Mark 7.24–30*, Biblical Tools and Studies, Vol. 11, Leuven: Peeters.

Archbishop of Canterbury's Commission on Urban Priority Areas, 1985, *Faith in the City: A Call for Action by Church and Nation*, London: Church House Publishing.

Ashmore, J., 2017, 'Norman Tebbit does not like being told to get on his bike', *Total Politics*, www.totalpolitics.com/articles/news/norman-tebbit-does-not-being-told-get-his-bike, accessed 23.10.20.

Atkinson, B., Coate, J., Fitzgerald, R., Furness, G., McClellan, P., Milroy, H. and Murray, A., 2017, *Royal Commission into Institutional Responses to Child Sexual Abuse*, www.childabuseroyalcommission. gov.au/final-report, accessed 23.10.20.

Baramosy, S., 2018, *Kenotic Ecclesiology*, Cairo, Egypt: Alexandria School.

Barth, K., Bromiley, G. W. and Torrance, T. F., 1958, *Church Dogmatics, Vol. IV, The Doctrine of Reconciliation, Part 2*, Edinburgh: T&T Clark.

BBC News, 2008, 'Map Highlights "Obesity Hotspots"', www.news. bbc.co.uk/1/hi/health/7584191.stm, accessed 23.10.20.

BBC News, 2016, 'EU Referendum: The result in maps and charts', www.bbc.co.uk/news/uk-politics-36616028, accessed 23.10.20.

Beaumont, S., 2019, *How to Lead When You Don't Know Where You are Going: Leading in a Liminal Season*, Lanham MD: Rowman & Littlefield.

Bonhoeffer, D., 2012, *The Collected Sermons of Dietrich Bonhoeffer*, Minneapolis, MN: Fortress Press.

Bonzo, J. M. and Stevens, M. R., 2008, *Wendell Berry and the Cultivation of Life: A Reader's Guide*, Grand Rapids, MI/ Oxford: Brazos.

Brown, D., 2011, *Divine Humanity: Kenosis and the Construction of a Christian Theology*, Waco TX: Baylor.

Burton, T. I., 2020, *Strange Rites: New Religions for a Godless World*, New York: Hachette/Public Affairs.

Burrows, M., 2016, ed., *The Paraclete Poetry Anthology*, Orleans, MA: Paraclete Press.

Cairns, S. Scott, 2019, 'Late Sayings', in *Anaphora: New Poems*, Orleans, MA: Paraclete Press; and Mark Burrows, ed., 2015, *The Paraclete Poetry Anthology*, Orleans, MA: Paraclete Press.

Camus, A., 1991, *The Plague*, trans. Gilbert, S., New York: Vintage.

Carlile, L., 2017, *Bishop George Bell – The Independent Review*, www.churchofengland.org/sites/default/files/2017-12/Bishop%20 George%20Bell%20-%20The%20Independent%20Review.pdf, accessed 15.12.2017.

Carrette, J. R. and King, R., 2005, *Selling Spirituality: The Silent Takeover of Religion*, London: Routledge.

Carter Florence, Anna, 2018, *Rehearsing Scripture: Discovering God's Word in Community*, London: Canterbury Press, 2018.

Cokcayne, E., 2020, *Rummage: A History of the Things We Have Reused, Recycled and Refused to Let Go*, London: Polity Press.

Collins, J., 2001, 'Level 5 Leadership: The Triumph of Humility and Fierce Resolve', *Harvard Business Review*, 79(1), pp. 66–76.

Collins, S., 2000, 'Spirituality and Youth', in Percy, M., ed., *Calling Time: Religion and Change at the Turn of the Millennium*, Sheffield: Sheffield Academic Press, pp. 221–37.

Connor, T., 2011, *The Kenotic Trajectory of the Church in Donald MacKinnon's Theology*, London: Bloomsbury.

Colquhoun, F., 1996, *Paris Prayers*, London: Hodder & Stoughton.

Cox, H., 1968, *On Not Leaving it to the Snake*, London: SCM Press.

Davie, G., 1994, *Religion in Britain since 1945: Believing Without Belonging. Making Contemporary Britain*, Oxford: Blackwell.

Davie, G., 2013, *Religion in Britain: A Persistent Paradox*, Oxford: Blackwell.

Davis, A., 2011, 'Autumn Awakening', in *Issues of Race, Poverty and the Environment*, vol. 18, 2, p. 4.

Dean, K. C., 2010, *Almost Christian: What the Faith of our Teenagers is Telling the American Church*, Oxford/New York: Oxford University Press.

Debuyst, F., 1968, *Modern Christian Architecture and Christian Celebration*, London: Lutterworth.

Donovan, V. J., 1982, *Christianity Rediscovered: An Epistle from the Masai*, London: SCM Press.

Filby, E., 2015, *God & Mrs Thatcher: The Battle for Britain's Soul*, London: Biteback Publishing.

Flory, R. W. and Miller, D. E., 2000, *GenX Religion*, New York/ London: Routledge.

Fuller, R., 2001, *Spiritual But Not Religious: Understanding Unchurched America*, Oxford: Oxford University Press.

Gibb, M., 2017, *The Independent Peter Ball Review – An Abuse of Faith*, www.churchofengland.org/sites/default/files/2017-11/report-of-the-peter-ball-review-210617.pdf, accessed 21.6.2017.

Gilmore, J. and Pine, J., 1998, 'Welcome to the Experience Economy', *Harvard Business Review* (July–August), pp. 12–15.

Gilmore, J. and Pine, J., 1999, *The Experience Economy: Work is Theatre & Every Business a Stage*, Boston, MA: Harvard Business School Press.

Gortner, D., 2013, *Varieties of Personal Theology: Charting the Beliefs and Values of American Young Adults*, London: Ashgate.

Greenleaf, R. K., 1991, *Servant Leadership: A Journey into the Nature of Legitimate Power and Greatness*, New York: Paulist Press.

Hafiz, 1999, *The Gift – Poems by Hafiz the Great Sufi Master*, trans. Ladninsky, D., London: Penguin.

Hardy, D.W., 1989, 'Created and Redeemed Sociality', in Hardy, C. G. D., ed., *On Being the Church: Essays on the Christian Community*, Edinburgh: T. & T. Clark.

Hardy, D. W. and Ford, D. F., 1984, *Jubilate: Theology in Praise*, London: Darton, Longman and Todd.

Hare, D., 2009, *The Power of Yes: A Dramatist Seeks to Understand the Financial Crisis*, London: Faber and Faber.

Hartnell, J., 2018, *Medieval Bodies: Life, Death and Art in the Middle Ages*, London: Wellcome Collection.

Hatcher, J., 2008, *The Black Death: An Intimate History*, London: Weidenfeld and Nicolson.

Hauerwas, S., 2013, *A Community of Character: Toward a Constructive Christian Social Ethic. Twentieth Century Religious Thought, Volume I: Christianity*, Notre Dame, IN: University of Notre Dame Press.

Heelas, P., 2005, *The Spiritual Revolution: Why Religion is Giving Way to Spirituality. Religion and Spirituality in the Modern World*, Malden, MA/Oxford: Blackwell.

Herman, J., 1992, *Trauma and Recovery: The Aftermath of Violence from Domestic Abuse to Political Terror*, Boston: Beacon Books.

Hervieu-Léger, D., 2000, *Religion as a Chain of Memory*, Cambridge: Polity Press.

Hill, C., 1972, *The World Turned Upside Down: Radical Ideas During the English Revolution*, London: Temple Smith.

Horton, R., 2020, *The COVID-19 Catastrophe*, London: Polity Press.

Howe, N. and Strauss, W., 2000, *Millennials Rising: The Next Great Generation*, New York: Vintage Books.

IICSA., 2019, *Child Sexual Abuse in the Anglican Church*. www.iicsa. org.uk/investigations/investigation-into-failings-by-the-anglican-church?tab=summary, accessed 6.10.2020.

Iqbal, N., 2018, 'Generation Z', *The Observer*, www.theguardian. com/society/2018/jul/21/generation-z-has-different-attitudes-says-a-new-report, accessed 1.2.2021.

Jamieson, A., 2002, *A Churchless Faith: Faith Journeys Beyond the Churches*, London: SPCK.

Jeavens, C., 2014, 'In Maps: How Close Was the Scottish Referendum Vote?', *BBC News*, www.bbc.co.uk/news/uk-scotland-scotland-poli tics-29255449, accessed 19.9.2014.

Kushner, H. S., 1981, *When Bad Things Happen to Good People*, London: Pan.

Lapierre, D. and Spink, K., 1986, *The City of Joy*, London: Arrow.

Lehman, D., ed., 2006, *The Oxford Book of American Poetry*, Oxford: Oxford University Press, p. 184.

Lodewyke, S., 2020 'Other', unpublished poem.

Lynch, C., 2019, *Ecclesial Leadership as Friendship. Explorations in Practical, Pastoral and Empirical Theology*, London: Routledge.

Lynch, T., 1998, *The Undertaking: Life Studies from the Dismal Trade*, London: Vintage.

Lynch, T., 2003, 'Good Grief: An Undertaker's Reflections', *The Christian Century*, https://christiancentury.org/article/2003-07/good-grief, accessed 26.7.2003.

MacIntyre, A. C., 1999, *Dependent Rational Animals: Why Human Beings Need the Virtues*, London: Duckworth.

MacKinnon, D., 1993, 'Reflections on Donald Baillie's Treatment of the Atonement', in Fergusson, D., ed., *Christ, Church and Society: Essays on John Baillie and Donald Baillie*. Edinburgh: T & T Clark, pp. 115–21.

MacKinnon, D. and Kirkland, S., 2011, *Philosophy and the Burden of Theological Honesty: A Donald MacKinnon Reader*, London: T&T Clark.

MacKinnon, D. M., 1969, *The Stripping of the Altars: The Gore Memorial Lecture Delivered on 5 November 1968 in Westminster Abbey and Other Papers and Essays on Related Topics*, London: Collins; Fontana.

MacMurray, J., 1970, *Persons in Relation*, London: Faber & Faber.

McDowell, J., Kirkland, S. and Moyise, A., eds, 2016, *Kenotic Ecclesiology: Selected Writings of Donald MacKinnon*, Augsburg MN: Fortress Press.

McGarrah Sharp, M. A., 2020, *Creating Resistances: Pastoral Care in a Postcolonial World*, Leiden: Brill.

McGrath, M., 1995, *Motel Nirvana: Dreaming of the New Age in the American Desert*, London: HarperCollins.

McKinsey & Company, 2012, *Women Matter 2012: Making the Breakthrough*, www.mckinsey.com, accessed 22.10.20.

Markham, I. and Daniel, J., eds, 2018, *Reasonable Radical?: Reading the Writings of Martyn Percy*, Eugene, OR: Pickwick Publications.

Moltmann, J., ed., 1978, *The Open Church: Invitation to a Messianic Lifestyle*, London: SCM Press.

Morgan, D., 2018, *Snobbery*, Cambridge: Polity Press.

Morris, J. A., Brotheridge, C. M. and Urbanski, J. C., 2005, 'Bringing Humility to Leadership: Antecedents and Consequences of Leader Humility', *Human Relations*, 58, pp. 1323–50.

Mortimer, I., 2009, *The Time Traveller's Guide to Medieval England: A Handbook for Visitors to the Fourteenth Century*, London: Vintage.

Myers, D. and Scanzoni, L., 2005, *What God Has Joined Together?* San Francisco: Harper.

Niebuhr, H., 1929, *The Social Sources of Denominationalism*, New York: Henry Holt & Co.

Nielsen, R., Marrone, J. and Slay, H., 2010, 'A New Look at Humility: Exploring the Humility Concept and its Role in Socialized Charismatic Leadership', *Journal of Leadership & Organizational Studies*, 17 (1), pp. 33–43.

Noddings, N., 1984, *Caring: A Feminine Approach to Ethics & Moral Education*, Berkeley: University of California Press.

Noddings, N., 2002, *Educating Moral People: A Caring Alternative to Character Education*, New York: Teachers College Press.

Oladipo, O., 2020, 'I Cannot Breathe', www.wycliffe.ox.ac.uk/article/death-george-floyd. Used with permission and with many thanks.

Oliver, M., 2007, 'The Uses of Sorrow' in *Thirst*, Boston: Beacon Press.

Parks, S. D., 2011, *Big Questions, Worthy Dreams: Mentoring Emerging Adults in their Search for Meaning, Purpose, and Faith*, San Francisco/Chichester: Jossey-Bass.

Pencavel, H., 2001, 'Roadbuilding', in *Shine On, Star of Bethlehem: A Worship Resource for Advent, Christmas and Epiphany*, compiled by Geoffrey Duncan, Norwich: Canterbury Press.

Percy, E., unpublished poems: 'Another Economy', 2019; 'The Body of Christ', 2017; 'Breathe', 2020; 'The Elephant in the Room', 2020; 'Kyrie Eleison', 2020; 'Room', 2019. All poems used with permission and with thanks.

Percy, M., 1997, 'Consecrated Pragmatism', *Anvil* 14(1), pp. 18–28.

Percy, M., 2000, *Calling Time: Religion and Change at the Turn of the Millennium. Lincoln Studies in Religion and Society*, Sheffield: Sheffield Academic Press.

Percy, M., 2001, *The Salt of the Earth: Religious Resilience in a Secular Age. Lincoln Studies in Religion and Society*, Sheffield: Sheffield Academic Press.

Percy, M., 2003, 'Mind the Gap: Generational Change and Its Implications for Mission', in Avis, P., ed., *Public Faith: The State of Religious Belief and Practice in Britain*, London: SPCK, pp. 92–105.

Percy, M., 2013, 'Easter Sermon, "More Than Tongues Can Tell"', delivered at Christchurch Cathedral, New Zealand, reprinted in Anglican Taonga, May 2013.

Percy. M., 2017a, 'Restoration, Retrieval and Renewal: Recovering Healing Ministry in the Church – Some Critical Reflections', in Sarisky D., ed., *Theologies of Retrieval: Practices and Perspectives*, London: Bloomsbury and T & T Clark.

Percy, M., 2017b, 'The Household of Faith', in Guyer, P. A. B., ed., *The Lambeth Conference: Theology, History, Polity and Purpose*, London/ New York: Bloomsbury T & T Clark, pp. 316–40.

Percy, M., 2018, 'Passionate Coolness; Exploring Mood and Character in Ecclesial Polity', in Lemons, J. D. (ed.), *Theologically Engaged Anthropology*, Oxford: Oxford University Press, pp. 296–314.

Percy. M., 1996, *Words, Wonders and Power: Understanding Contemporary Christian Fundamentalism and Revivalism*, London: SPCK.

Percy, M. and Ward, P. 2014, *The Wisdom of the Spirit: Gospel, Church and Culture*, Farnham, Surrey/Burlington, VT: Ashgate.

Pew Research Center, 2014, *Report on America's Religious Landscape*, www.pewforum.org/2015/05/12/americas-changing-religious-landscape/, accessed 12.5.2015.

Perez, C. C., 2019, *Invisible Women: Exposing Data Bias in a World Designed for Men*, London: Chatto & Windus.

Peterson, E. H. 1992, *Under the Unpredictable Plant: An Exploration in Vocational Holiness*. Grand Rapids, MI: Eerdmans.

Plowright, P., 'Choosing', *The Tablet*, 17 January 2019, p. 12.

Putnam, R. D., 2000, *Bowling Alone: The Collapse and Revival of American Community*, New York/London: Simon & Schuster.

Putnam, R. D., 2015, *Our Kids: The American Dream in Crisis*, New York: Simon & Schuster.

Reeves, D., 1996, *Down to Earth: A New Vision for the Church*, London: Mowbray.

Robinson, J. A. T., 1965, *The New Reformation? Purdy Lectures, 1964*, London: SCM Press.

Roof, W. C. and Greer, B., 1993, *A Generation of Seekers: The Spiritual Journeys of the Baby Boom Generation*, San Francisco: Harper.

Roof, W. C. and McKinney, W., 1987, *American Mainline Religion: Its Changing Shape and Future*, New Brunswick, NJ/London: Rutgers University Press.

Saliba, J. A., 1999, *Christian Responses to the New Age Movement: A Critical Assessment*, London: Geoffrey Chapman.

Sandel, M., 2020, *The Tyranny of Merit*, London: Penguin.

Sargeant, K., 2000, *Seeker Churches: Promoting Traditional Religion in a Nontraditional Way*, New Brunswick, NJ: Rutgers University Press.

Selby, P., 1991, *BeLonging: Challenge to A Tribal Church*, London: SPCK.

Shakespeare, T., 2014, 'A Point of View: Is it better to be religious than spiritual?', *BBC Magazine*, www.bbc.co.uk/news/magazine-27554640, accessed 24.5.2014.

Smart, H., 1995, 'Praise', in *A Fool's Pardon*, London: Faber & Faber, p. 7.

Snowden, F. M., 2019, *Epidemics and Society: From the Black Death to the Present*, New Haven, CA: Yale University Press.

Spector, T., 2020, *Spoon-Fed: Why Almost Everything We Have Been Told About Food is Wrong*, London: Jonathan Cape.

Tavris, C. and Aronson, E., 2008, *Mistakes Were Made (But Not by Me): Why We Justify Foolish Beliefs, Bad Decisions, and Hurtful Acts*, Orlando: Harvest Books.

Tawney, R. H. and Seligman, A. B., 2017, *Religion and the Rise of Capitalism*, Abingdon: Taylor & Francis.

Taylor, J. V., 1972, *The Go-Between God: The Holy Spirit and the Christian Mission*, London: SCM Press.

Tetlock, P. and Gardner, D., 2016, *Superforecasting: The Art and Science of Prediction*, London: Random House.

Thatcher, M., 1987, Interview for *Woman's Own* ('no such thing as society'), in Keay, D., ed., *Woman's Own*.

Toynbee, P., 2017, 'Brexiteers call it useless red tape, but without it people die', *Guardian*, www.theguardian.com/commentisfree/2017/jun/20/brexiteers-red-tape-people-die-boris-johnson-grenfell-tower, accessed 20.6.2017.

Underhill, Evelyn, 1990, 'God is the Interesting Thing', *The Christian Century*, 19 October.

Vanstone, W. H., 1977, *Love's Endeavour, Love's Expense: The Response of Being to the Love of God*, London: Darton, Longman and Todd. pp. 108–9.

Vanstone, W. H., 1982, *The Stature of Waiting*, London: Darton, Longman and Todd.

von Moltke, H. J., 1991, *Letter to Freya: A Witness Against Hitler*, London: Collins-Harvill, pp. 410–11.

Wells, S., 2019, *Walk Humbly: Encouragements of Living, Working, and Being*, Norwich: Canterbury Press.

Whipp, M., 2017, *The Grace of Waiting*, Norwich: Canterbury Press.

Wilder, T, 1927, *The Bridge of San Luis Rey*, New York: Albert and Charles Boni.

Williams, J., 2020, *Ecclesianarchy: Adaptive Ministry for a Post-Church Society*, London: SCM Press.

Williams, J., 2018a *The Merciful Humility of God: The 2019 Lent Book*, London: Bloomsbury Continuum.

Williams, J., 2018b, *Seeking the God Beyond: A Beginner's Guide to Christian Apophatic Spirituality*, London: SCM Press.

Wilkerson, I., 2020, *Caste: The Lies That Divide Us*, London: Allen Lane.

Winstanley, G., 1649, *A Watch-Word to the City of London, and the Armie*, Lond: Lond.

Wyatt, T., 2016, 'Survivors Protest aided by Chapter', *Church Times*, www.churchtimes.co.uk/articles/2016/7-october/news/uk/survivors-protest-aided-by-chapter, 7 October.

Zaidi, M., 2020, *A Dutiful Boy: A Memoir of a Gay Muslim's Journey to Acceptance*, London: Vintage Books.

Zorgdrager, H., 2017, 'Risk-Takers in a World that Cries for Salvation: Behr-Sigel on Suffering and Kenosis', in Hinlicky, S. and Pekridou, A., *A Communion of Love: Elisabeth Behr-Sigel's Ecclesiology*, Geneva: WCC, pp. 127–39.

Endnotes and Further Reading

1 Although not a phrase used by the author, I warmly commend Carter Florence (2018), *Rehearsing Scripture*.

2 On the history of rubbish and recycling, see Cokcayne (2020), *Rummage*.

3 Evelyn Underhill in a private letter she wrote to Archbishop Cosmo Gordon Lang of Canterbury, 1930.

4 From a 'Letter to the editor' in the print version of *The Economist*, 2 May 2020, p. 12.

5 www.covidlive.co.uk/.

6 A British grassroots political organization founded in 2015 which is supportive of the Labour Party.

7 The Fresh Expressions movement began in 2004 following a report prepared by an ecumenical group and published by the Church of England which suggested that there should be recognition and provision for those seeking to work with changing culture and those not yet attending church, http://freshexpressions.org.uk/about/, accessed 29.5.19.

8 See: https://remembermeproject.wordpress.com/the-project/, accessed 26.5.19.

9 'Send her away' is my preferred rendering of the Greek text. However, the RNJB opts for 'Give her what she wants'. While this is construable for the first half of this verse, the majority of translations tend to opt for the form of words I have put in brackets, as the disciples clearly wish to banish her from their presence for being a noisy and disruptive nuisance.

10 In the Greek the term is the same, *kunaria*.

11 Remember that Jesus called Herod a 'fox' – a sneaky scavenger that preys on the vulnerable. For a good discussion of canine pedigree and humanity, see Alizart, 2020, *Dogs*.

12 We note the renewed interest in this field. For example, see Connor (2011), *The Kenotic Trajectory of the Church*; Brown (2011), *Divine Humanity*; Baramosy (2018), *Kenotic Ecclesiology*; McDowell, Kirkland and Moyise, eds (2016), *Kenotic Ecclesiology: Selected Writings of Donald MacKinnon*.

13 However, see also Whipp (2017), *The Grace of Waiting*. Whipp argues for the virtue of watchful patience as one of the primary disciplines to be cultivated in addressing suffering, as well as discussing the shortcomings of stoicism.

14 For a discussion of this that pays attention to gender, see Zorgdrager (2017), 'Risk-Takers in a World that Cries for Salvation'.

15 Readers may be interested in exploring the memoir by Mohsin Zaidi (2020), *A Dutiful Boy*, in which the author writes movingly of the primacy of love in overcoming the hurt he encountered from family, friends and community as a gay man, and how love healed and restored relationships that had been broken.

16 www.churchtimes.co.uk/articles/2017/11-august/news/uk/church-is-abandoning-the-poorest-areas-bishop-warns, accessed 11.8. 2017.

17 Niebuhr argued that Protestantism's fondness for all things related to growth and capitalism had led to the triumph of individualistic rather than collective concerns. His discussion of how denominations dealt with the issues of slavery and partial secession from the USA is particularly insightful. Churches that had begun as movements of the dispossessed with an emphasis on equality (Methodists and the Baptists for example) condemned slavery, while the denominations that had been exported to the USA as offshoots of European state churches (Episcopalians and Lutherans for example) were less inclined to defy the temporal order, and often defended the state. With slave-ownership and politics all entwined within religion, the Confederate–Union division of the American Civil War (1861–65) split denominations too. Episcopalians in the Northern states did little to challenge the views of their slave-owning counterparts in the Southern states. Baptists in the South then split on racial lines as much as theological. African American churches emerged as their members chose self-determination rather than having inferior status and roles in 'integrated' churches, still riddled with classism and racism. Niebuhr's book was driven by his sociological imagination, and his attempt to persuade Christians to acknowledge the secular roots and character of their denominations. He believed this was necessary to achieve Christian unity, which would lead the churches closer to Christ's vision of the Kingdom of God.

18 For further reading, I commend Vanstone (1982), *The Stature of Waiting*; and Whipp (2017), *The Grace of Waiting*.

Acknowledgement of Sources

The author and publisher are grateful to the following publishers and individuals for permission to use poetry under copyright.

Anna Akhmatova, 2006, *Anna Akhmatova: Poems*, trans. D. M. Thomas, New York: Knopf.

S. Scott Cairns, 2015, 'Late Sayings', in *Slow Pilgrim: Collected Poems*, Orleans, MA: Paraclete Press.

Hafiz, 1991, *The Gift: Poems by Hafiz the Great Sufi Master*, trans. D. Ladninsky, London: Penguin.

Emma Lazarus, 2006, 'The New Colossus', in D. Lehman, ed., *The Oxford Book of American Poetry*, Oxford: Oxford University Press.

Steve Lodewyke, 'Otherness', unpublished poem used by permission of the author.

Oyin Olipado, 'I Cannot Breathe', unpublished poem used by permission of the author.

Mary Oliver, 2007, 'The Uses of Sorrow', in *Thirst: Poems*, Boston: Beacon Press.

Heather Pencavel, 'Roadbuilding', unpublished poem used by permission of the author.

Emma Percy, 'Another Economy', 'The Body of Christ', 'Breathe', 'The Elephant in the Room', 'Kyrie Eleison' and 'Room', unpublished poems used by permission of the author.

Piers Plowright, 2019, 'Choosing', in *The Tablet*, 17 January 2019.

Harry Smart, 1995, 'Praise', in *A Fool's Pardon*, London: Faber & Faber.

W. H. Vanstone, 2007, 'Morning Story, Starlit Sky', in *Love's Endeavour, Love's Expense: The Response of Being to the Love of God*, London: Darton, Longman and Todd.

Index of Names and Subjects

Acts 115
American Civil War 102

Baillie, Donald 137
Baldwin, James 158-9
Ball, Peter 77, 85
Barth, Karl 24
Bell, George 77
Bellah, Robert 119
Berry, Wendell 25
Bills of Mortality 33, 35
Black Lives Matter 30
Brexit 46, 52, 165
Buddha 55

Cameron, David 81
Camus, Albert 35-6, 40
Carnegie, Dale 157
Charles I 105
Charles II 33
Christ Church, Oxford 33,
    50-1, 75, 166
Civil Rights Movement 158
Collins, Jim 53-4
Corinthians 14, 156
Covid-19 (C-19) 11, 13,
    34-5, 37-8, 49-50, 52-3,
    56, 131-2, 149

Davie, Grace 64
Davis, Angela 162
Dickens, Charles 167
Donovan, Vincent 124-5

Ebola 34
Eliot, T. S. 84
English Revolution 27, 105

Galatians 99
Gandhi, Mahatma 156
Gender xv, 4, 11, 19, 63, 65,
    85, 90-4, 97-8, 101-2,
    120, 123-4, 129, 131,
    158, 161, 165
Generation X 62, 65
Generation Z/ Z-ers 62-6,
    72, 74
Genesis 57
Greenleaf, Robert 137
Grenfell 81-2

Hafiz 21, 121-2
Handsworth and Brixton
    Riots 49
Hare, David 48-9
Herbert, George 160
HIV 34

Industrial Revolution 67

James 143
John xii, 1–4, 39, 122, 134, 144,149
John the Baptist 87

Kempe, Margery 154
Kushner, Harold 40–1

Lambeth Conference 23, 120
Lapierre, Dominique 125
Leprosy 50–1
Letter of James 134
Leviticus 50
Lewis, C. S. 117, 189
LGBTQ+ Community 61, 108, 119, 124
Luke 7, 24, 29, 37, 39, 45, 87, 115, 147, 152–3, 163, 165, 170

MacIntyre, Alasdair 43
MacKinnon, Donald 137–8
MacMurray, John 40
Mark 108, 185
Matthew 25, 101, 108–9, 111, 115, 147
Micah 1
Millennials 62, 65–6, 71–2, 74
Momentum 64
Moses 55, 148
Muhammad 55

NHS 38, 45–6
Noddings, Nel 78

Orwell, George 161

Pandemic 11, 28, 33–5, 37–8, 41, 43, 45–6, 50, 53, 131–2, 142, 149–50
Parable of the Good Samaritan 29–30, 37, 76, 112–13, 170
Pepys, Samuel 50
Peter 143
Petersen, Eugene 25
Philippians xii, 2–3, 8, 15, 136
Plague 33–6, 45
Plowright, Piers 171–2
Psalms 3

Robinson, John 125
Royal Commission into Institutional Responses to Child Sexual Abuse 77–8

Saint Augustine 157
Samaritans (Charity) 28, 37, 126
Sexuality xv, 15, 23, 63, 85, 90, 93, 120, 123, 129, 131, 133, 158, 161–2, 165
Shakespeare, William 50

Taylor, John V. 121
Thatcher, Margaret 5, 47–9
Titus 152
Tutu, Desmond 84, 157
Twin Towers 65

Underhill, Evelyn 23, 175

Vanstone, William Hubert
  15–16, 144
Varah, Chad 28, 37, 45, 126

Wells, H. G. 156
Wilder, Thornton 44–5

Winstanley, Gerard 27, 29
World Health Organization
  52

Zika 34